For over thirty years, the Harvard Institutes for Higher Education (HIHE) have been an important resource for the leadership of colleges and universities. HIHE offers world-renowned professional development programs, providing campus leaders with the information and insights necessary for personal and institutional success. All of these programs incorporate the use of case studies. HIHE regularly produces new case studies, to ensure that its teaching materials reflect the most current issues confronting campus leaders. HIHE maintains the country's largest collection of case studies in higher education administration. These case studies are used in professional development programs and in graduate-level courses in educational administration.

To request information on HIHE's professional development programs or to receive a current catalogue of case studies, please contact Harvard Institutes for Higher Education, 14 Story Street, 4th floor, Cambridge, MA 02138

Using Cases in Higher Education

A Guide for Faculty and Administrators

James P. Honan and
Cheryl Sternman Rule

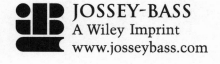
JOSSEY-BASS
A Wiley Imprint
www.josseybass.com

JOSSEY-BASS
A Wiley Imprint
www.josseybass.com

Published by Jossey-Bass
A Wiley Imprint
989 Market Street, San Francisco, CA 94103-1741   www.josseybass.com

Jossey-Bass books and products are available through most bookstores. To contact Jossey-
Bass directly call our Customer Care Department within the U.S. at 800-956-7739, outside the U.S. at 317-572-3986 or fax 317-572-4002.

Jossey-Bass also publishes its books in a variety of electronic formats. Some content that
appears in print may not be available in electronic books.

Library of Congress Cataloging-in-Publication Data
Honan, James P.
    Using cases in higher education : a guide for faculty and administrators / James P.
Homan and Cheryl Sternman Rule.— 1st ed.
        p.   cm.
Includes bibliographical references.
    ISBN 0-7879-5391-1 (alk. paper)
    1. College teaching.   2. Universities and colleges—Administration.   3. Case
method.   I. Rule, Cheryl Sternman.   II. Title.
    LB2331 .H62 2002
    378.1'25—dc21

                                                                        2002007588

Printed in the United States of America
FIRST EDITION
HB Printing   10 9 8 7 6 5 4 3 2 1

Contents

Preface

Colleges and universities are inordinately complex, multilayered organizations in which numerous constituents—students, faculty members, administrators, staff members, trustees, and alumni—interact with one another over a broad spectrum of issues in order to further the goals of higher education. Due to this complexity, and the sheer number of constituencies involved, teaching about the issues confronting higher education leaders poses special challenges. Teaching and learning with case studies can be an especially effective pedagogical approach for both capturing and bringing to life the issues simmering in this environment. Why? Only by describing situations as they have actually occurred, through the lenses of the actual faculty members or administrators who have experienced them, can we capture fully the nuances of a budget struggle, governance battle, or policy formulation dilemma. Faculty members who teach graduate courses in higher education administration and those who teach in various professional development institutes and executive education programs for experienced practitioners have increasingly made ample use of the case study method as an integral part of their pedagogy.

In an era when colleges and universities seek administrators who possess and exhibit exceptional problem-solving and leadership abilities, case studies constitute windows through which

academic leaders can observe and learn from administrative suc-
cesses and foibles on other campuses. Some college and university
administrators, even those with many years of experience, typically
approach problems in a "tried-and-true" way. By examining and discussing situations in which leaders have used novel problem-
solving techniques, these same administrators might be able to
move beyond comfortable responses and routines and envision new
ways of working and leading. Ideally, the glimpses that case study
discussions provide into others' strategies will help both current and
future academic leaders test new perspectives on a particular problem or dilemma and expand their own repertoires of administrative
skills and abilities.

Faculty members have grumbled for years about how raises are
awarded in the College of Engineering at a large urban university.
While aware of the simmering dissatisfaction for some time, the dean
has not known how to address the issue effectively. Until now, he has
ignored the problem, hoping that it would either go away on its own
or at least remain beneath the surface while other issues occupied
the faculty's overloaded agenda. While attending a summer institute
for midlevel managers, the dean read a case study detailing a similar
scenario at another university in the early 1990s. By reading the case
study, discussing it with his peers, and fleshing out, with the guidance and support of his institute colleagues, how he would broach
the issue on his own campus, the dean was emboldened to draft a
new workload and salary equity proposal to discuss with his faculty
members that fall.

This scenario represents just one way in which case studies can help
enlighten, inform, and inspire administrators to take a fresh
approach to campus problem solving and policy making.

When used well, case studies represent powerful pedagogical
tools to develop and strengthen an administrator's ability to ana-

lyze, assess, and respond to the complex and difficult issues facing today's higher education leaders and managers. Such issues cover a wide spectrum and run the gamut from overburdened junior faculty members to decreased state appropriations to the changing demographics of today's student bodies to concerns over faculty research protocols. The list of "hot" issues on today's campuses is truly endless. And the groups convening to address and confront these issues are just as numerous. Each of these groups—from boards of trustees to faculty workgroups to administrative committees—can, and many do, benefit from the use of case studies as a means to work through the tasks of solving problems, brainstorming new ideas, and planning for the future. Board retreats and campus planning sessions are just two of the many environments where case studies play a central role on a day- or weekend-long agenda. By collaborating with peers, with the guidance and encouragement of a case instructor, participants in case discussions can also test new ways of addressing administrative situations. Robust and focused discussions of cases, convened in a productive and constructive way, enable participants to reflect on administrative practice in higher education and to identify alternative ways to resolve a wide range of leadership problems and dilemmas.

Introduction
Teaching and Learning with Case Studies

This guide is designed to help faculty and administrators use case studies to illuminate and explore the many complex dilemmas facing higher education leaders. The advice and suggestions presented can apply equally well to a broad spectrum of cases, and this volume may be used with case studies of the instructor's choosing. The authors of this volume have also edited a collection of case studies entitled *Casebook I: Faculty Employment Policies* (Jossey-Bass, 2002). Teaching notes to these cases are also available in *Teaching Notes to Casebook I: Faculty Employment Policies* (Jossey-Bass, 2002).

Whereas this guide provides instructors and discussion leaders with general advice and insights regarding the use of case studies in higher education settings, the teaching notes accompanying each case study provide more detailed suggestions and strategies for leading an effective classroom or workshop discussion. Ideally, the guide and teaching notes are used together to help instructors use case studies in a variety of instructional settings, including graduate degree programs in higher education, professional development institutes, executive education programs and conferences, campus-based administrative and leadership seminars, and in-service workshops and retreats.

This guide is organized into four chapters. Chapter One provides an overview of the case study method, contrasts it with lecture-based instruction, describes the instructor's role in the case-teaching process, and outlines the numerous ways in which cases can enhance student and participant learning. Chapter Two provides a closer look at cases themselves: what specifically makes them effective teaching tools, how to select an appropriate case for a course or institute, and what criteria to employ when pairing cases with theoretical and supplementary readings. Chapter Three provides a detailed account of how to prepare for a case discussion, how to facilitate such a session, and how to conclude. And Chapter Four presents strategies for applying case learning to administrative practice beyond the classroom.

Each chapter contains several examples to illustrate the ideas under discussion. In addition, Chapters Three and Four also include examples from the teaching note to the Kansas State University case study. These points, all presented in boxes, provide the reader with a central reference point for the guide's advice and suggestions. The entire Kansas State University case is provided as an appendix to this volume. We strongly encourage you to familiarize yourself with it before moving on to the rest of this guide. Doing so will bring the examples to life and will further your understanding of the finer points of case method teaching and learning.

To help direct you to other publications on the case study method, this guide concludes with an annotated bibliography of useful resources.

1

Overview

Using Cases in Higher Education

The case study method is one of a number of pedagogical tools and approaches that faculty members in higher education administration courses and discussion leaders in leadership or management development programs have at their disposal. As with any pedagogical approach, case-based teaching and learning is characterized by particular purposes and principles. According to Barnes, Christensen, and Hansen (1994), case method teaching is grounded in five fundamental principles:

- The primacy of situational analysis

- The imperative of relating analysis and action

- The necessity of student involvement

- A nontraditional instructor role

- A balance of substantive and process teaching (pp. 47–49)

Argyris (1980) also offers five essential features of case method instruction:

- The use of actual problems

- Maximum participant involvement

- Minimal reliance on the instructor

- An absence of objective ("right" or "wrong") answers

- Instructor- and case-created drama into which participants are drawn (p. 291)

Both Barnes et al. and Argyris agree: analysis, action, a unique rapport between student and instructor, and active student involvement form the backbone of case method teaching and learning.

When used effectively, discussions of case studies enable instructors to energize the classroom environment and to engage participants with one another and with the theoretical and practice-oriented aspects of the case material. Through this medium, participants can systematically analyze and reflect on realistic, fact-based leadership and administrative dilemmas in a safe atmosphere while discussing, debating, and defending various points of view. As Hammond (1980) notes:

> Cases help managers sharpen their analytic skills, since they must produce quantitative and qualitative evidence to support recommendations and decisions. In case discussions, participants are challenged by their instructors and fellow participants to defend their arguments and analyses; the effect on the participant is a sharpening of problem-solving and a heightened ability to think and reason rigorously [p. 1].

Hammond adds: "The case method of learning does not provide the *answer*. Rather, several viable 'answers' will be developed and supported by various participants within the total group" (p. 3). McDade (1988) echoes this general view, noting that "a 'right' answer or 'correct solution' is rarely apparent" (p. 1) in a case discussion. Instructors should remind participants that the purpose of a case discussion is not to crack the case but rather to explore the multiple perspectives and interpretations of those administrative and leadership dilemmas that higher education administrators face in their day-to-day work.

Applegate (1988) underscores the point that cases are a means to a more fundamental instructional end: "It is only with experience that we learn that the case serves as a backdrop for enabling students to discover the specific concepts and skills the course is designed to teach" (p. 1).

Using a case study approach to the teaching of higher education administration can benefit both beginning graduate students and experienced administrators alike. This pedagogical approach enables instructors to expose graduate students in higher education degree programs to a wide range of administrative situations and dilemmas in their full complexity and within actual institution-based settings. Cases also provide students with an opportunity to explore "real-life" examples of how particular theories and analytical frameworks and research findings apply (or do not apply) to actual administrative practice. More experienced administrators of colleges and universities also have much to gain by participating in case-based courses, seminars, and professional development institutes. With their knowledge of and experience in handling multifaceted and often contentious campus-based predicaments, seasoned administrators can benefit from case discussions by gaining new perspectives and insights from their colleagues about how best to confront and tackle the many complex issues they regularly face in their work as academic leaders.

In many instances, participants in case discussions can learn as much from one another as they do from the instructor teaching the case study. As a result, it is important for the instructor to make every effort to tap into the experience and wisdom of case discussion participants to the greatest extent possible. Particular strategies for doing this are discussed later in this guide and in the teaching notes accompanying each case.

The use of case study pedagogy can also yield benefits for instructors themselves. Richard Elmore, a faculty member at the Harvard Graduate School of Education and veteran case teacher, offers a personal reason for his belief in the value of case teaching: "I use cases because they teach me about student learning; cases open a window into the minds of students. Cases have taught me how to observe and understand minds at work" (in Merseth, 1998, p. xii).

In addition to providing instructors with powerful insights into "minds at work," case teaching also challenges faculty members to maximize the potential learning that goes along with having students so actively engaged in the instructional process. At the conclusion of a typical case study session, many instructors report feeling a combination of "exhausted" and "exhilarated." The sense of exhaustion comes from the sharp focus and intense listening that is required of a case instructor. The exhilaration results from having played a role in a highly interactive and stimulating learning opportunity.

Students, too, find learning with cases fresh and engaging. Typical student comments on the use of case studies in graduate courses in higher education administration include:

"Through the micro lens of a particular case, we learn about more general trends and challenges."

"Cases help stimulate thinking."

"Cases were helpful in illuminating topics and solidifying my understanding of concepts."

"Cases enabled me to apply theoretical frameworks and concepts to more concrete examples."

"Cases are an excellent tool for understanding major concepts in a practical way."

Reactions such as these provide a sense of the potential impact that high quality case teaching and learning experiences can have on students.

A student in a master's degree program in higher education administration, Maria was taking four classes and an independent study during her first semester of graduate school. Her reading load was intense, and she simply had to decide before each class what she would have time to read and what would fall by the wayside. Current Issues in Higher Education was a case-based course, and she enjoyed grappling with the dilemmas presented in each case. Last week, she read a case about participatory planning processes at a liberal arts college. Though neither well-versed nor particularly interested in planning issues, she read the case carefully, knowing a lively discussion awaited her in class. That week, she and her classmates analyzed the case study, took on the roles of faculty member, dean, and vice president for academic affairs, and hashed out the players' effective and ineffective strategies. Maria now understands the importance of planning processes and is sensitive to the politics that may play out should she ever find herself part of one. She may not have read the unit on planning had it appeared in a textbook or article, but she read the case study in anticipation of the discussion she knew would await her in class.

For students and instructors alike, the ability of case studies to bring the world of practice into the classroom proves mutually beneficial.

Case Method Instruction Versus Lecture-Based Instruction

Faculty and discussion leaders who incorporate the case study method into their teaching offer various reasons for their enthusiasm for this type of pedagogy over more traditional, such as lecture-based, instructional methods and routes to learning. At their best, case studies can serve as the basis and focal point for productive, learning-oriented conversations of the many sometimes difficult and contentious administrative and managerial problems and issues confronting higher education leaders.

Barnes, Christensen, and Hansen (1994) observe that case teaching "puts the students in an active learning mode, challenges them to accept substantial responsibility for their own education, and gives them first-hand appreciation of, and experience with, the application of knowledge to practice" (pp. 3–4). Case-based teaching and learning also allows participants to consider multiple assessments of a single administrative problem or dilemma, builds students' confidence in the diagnosis of complex administrative problems, promotes a tolerance for ambiguity and complexity, forces students to generate nonobvious, alternative responses to difficult administrative problems, and challenges students to adopt an "action perspective"(Boehrer, undated). As noted previously, cases also enable instructors to bring to bear, and benefit from, other professionals' expertise, experience, and observations during the course of a case discussion. Finally, in contrast to lecture-based teaching and learning where students tend to examine a text, students working with cases can actually "engage in the text," making their learning experience more interactive (Boehrer and Linsky, 1990) and imagining themselves taking part in a real-life scenario. The reader is no longer a passive observer but is transformed into an active participant. As a student in a case-based graduate school class in higher education administration observed, "Case studies really bring the readings to life and help us to synthesize concepts by placing them in a real world context."

Wassermann (1994) notes that the route to learning represents another essential contrast between traditional learning and the learning inspired by the case method. She observes that traditional, lecture-based teaching and learning follow "a linear progression, with a beginning, middle, and end [and] the purpose of the journey along the linear pathway seems concerned with the destination— that is, students' acquisition of specific knowledge" (p. 84). By contrast, the case learning pathway, according to Wassermann:

is far from linear. It folds over upon itself, backs up, returns to retrace steps, in a series of many investigatory stops along the pathway. . . . Along this more zig-zag learning pathway are a series of interrelated experiences that allow for the reframing of personal meanings, so that students are continually challenged to add each new life experience to their developing cognitive frameworks and deepening understandings [p. 84].

Because students are such active participants in a case study discussion, it is essential that they be well prepared for their multiple roles as listeners, advocates, skeptics, and naysayers. This preparation takes many forms and can be, to say the least, time consuming. Instructors and discussion leaders using case studies should highlight this issue for all participants—the "you get out of it what you put into it" adage certainly holds true. In fact, an instructor would be well advised to give participants a brief overview at the outset of the course or institute and to inform them up front of what will be expected of them in terms of preparation time and the extent to which case studies play a role in the course.

In the syllabus to Organizational Change in Higher Education, Professor Richard Chait of the Harvard Graduate School of Education informs his students about the role of case studies in his course. "Relying largely on case studies, the course applies different frameworks and theories to examine the change process, to analyze organizational problems, and to develop constructive strategies for change. The course rests on the assumption that effective administrators must be able to analyze complex problems, constructively change organizations, communicate effectively, work collaboratively, and make sense of ambiguity and uncertainty through an understanding of organizational theory." Later in the syllabus, Chait notes: "Classroom discussions will center on nonfictional case studies and supplemental readings." He also underscores that the course relies "heavily on classroom participation and collaboration" and that "contributions in class should reveal a substantial familiarity with assigned readings, a capacity to analyze the issues and problems under discussion, and an ability to listen to, incorporate, synthesize, and constructively criticize the comments and work of classmates."

At a minimum, students or participants should be asked to read the case study at least once (preferably more than once) before the discussion. Typically, an instructor will also assign supplementary readings to accompany the case study. Such readings might highlight research findings or theoretical frameworks pertinent to the topic or dilemma upon which the case study focuses. Needless to say, a participant who has not done any advance preparation for a case study discussion is unlikely to find the experience to be productive.

Despite emphasizing the need for reading and reflection in advance of a case discussion, there are instances where the instructor may occasionally have to orchestrate a discussion among students or institute participants who did not adequately prepare. If the instructor senses that there has been minimal (or no) advance preparation for the discussion, he or she may have to make fairly rapid adjustments, such as having participants take a few minutes to read (or reread) the case, discussing the case in small groups of two to six, or revising the teaching plan so that the case plays a less prominent role in the session and the role of relevant theory or supporting readings is emphasized instead. In situations such as this, the instructor should remind participants of the crucial role that advance preparation plays in an effective case discussion.

The Instructor's Role in Case Teaching

The case teacher or discussion leader is "planner, host, moderator, devil's advocate, fellow-student, and judge—a potentially confusing set of roles" (Barnes, Christensen, and Hansen, 1994, p. 23).

While teachers, faculty members, and instructors of all stripes have numerous styles and pedagogical approaches, the case teacher's function in the classroom remains somewhat unique.

In more traditional, lecture-based teaching, instructors serve primarily as purveyors of information and, to a certain extent, "experts" in the given subject matter. The "sage on the stage" metaphor has commonly been used to characterize this approach to teaching. A case teacher's primary function, by contrast, is to act as a skilled facilitator, breaking down barriers among students, making case discussions lively, and keeping the class on track. The traditional classroom hierarchy breaks down as instructors relegate control to students (Applegate, 1988). Applegate adds: "Traditional student-teacher roles, with their emphasis on hierarchy, are abandoned. Students assume responsibility for the learning environment" (p. 2). Boehrer (1996) agrees, noting that the students and teacher share "intellectual and procedural authority" during a case discussion (p. 1). Christensen (1991, in Barnes et al., 1994), widely regarded as one of the foremost experts on case teaching methodology, describes the unusual relationship among case teachers and students as a "partnership" and the class as a "learning community" (p. 25). He elaborates:

> Effective discussion leadership, unlike lecturing, requires instructors to forge a primary alliance with students. We do not bring the material to them, but rather help them find their own ways to it. The subject matter defines the boundaries of our intellectual territory, but the students' unique intellects, personalities, learning styles, fears, and aspirations shape the paths they will take [p. 28].

Because the case teacher's role is unique, students, too, play a special role in relation to one another and their instructor. This somewhat unique classroom environment and the learning generated within it share little in common with what is generally found in standard, lecture-based settings.

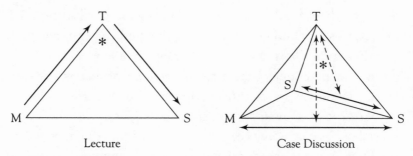

Lecture   Case Discussion

Figure 1.1. Comparison of the Functional Relationships Between Teacher, Students, and Course Material in Lecture and Case Discussion. *Source:* "How to Teach a Case." From the note written by John Boehrer, Kennedy School of Government, copyright © 1995 by the President and Fellows of Harvard College, © 1996 by the Cascade Center for Public Service. Reprinted with the permission of the Kennedy School of Government Case Program, Harvard University, and the Cascade Center for Public Service, Daniel J. Evans School of Public Affairs, University of Washington.

As shown in Figure 1.1, Boehrer (1996) has created an effective schematic to illustrate the contrasting relationships among teacher, students, and case material in both a lecture- and case-based setting.

The teacher (T) stands between the material (M) and the students (S) in lecture. In case discussion, the students meet the material more directly, and they interact with each other as well. Teaching a case consists of managing those encounters toward purposeful ends and (as the two <—> lines suggest) of learning from them as well, about both the students and the case itself. While intellectual and procedural authority (*) belongs to the teacher in the lecture, teacher and students share it in case discussion. Both determine what is learned, and students, as well as teachers, can raise questions. As the scheme for case discussion suggests, the exercise is significantly more challenging and interesting.

The following activity can drive home the point that students in a case-based discussion have genuine authority.

Activity: Invite participants to picture themselves in the role of consultant to the case protagonist. The instructor should pose general questions such as: How would you advise the decision maker in this case? Which options are more desirable than others? Why? Alternatively, the instructor can invite the participants to convene small teams of consultants who would be asked to offer suggestions and recommendations to the decision makers in the case.

By taking on the role of experts, participants learn to value their own contributions and to see how their ideas would or would not play out successfully in practice.

Using Cases to Promote Student Learning in Multiple Ways

Students in higher education administration courses and related degree programs, and administrators who take part in case study discussions in executive education programs and professional development institutes, can learn from case studies in several ways. First, individual reading of and reflection on a particular case study enable participants to gain knowledge of both common and unusual administrative dilemmas in the higher education work environment: How does institution X handle the evaluation of tenured faculty? How does institution Y deal with budget shortfalls? When well-written, case studies can capture the complexity and context of the higher education environment, its multiple players (among them presidents, deans, department chairs, faculty members, students, and trustees), and long-ingrained conflicts and challenges (assessment, tenure, governance, student versus administrative versus faculty wants and needs, budget and finance strategies, and so on). Second, informal pre- and post-case discussion interactions with colleagues encourage participants to share not only their interpretations of the particular case study but also the expertise and knowledge they bring to the table from their personal and professional experiences. Finally, the case discussion itself, of course, provides one of the most valuable and powerful opportunities for learning. It is here where the instructor and the discussion participants collectively attempt to untangle the case study's multiple threads and analyze and assess its larger themes. An instructor's overall pedagogical goal in making any case discussion experience part of a course should be to maximize all of these opportunities to create a rich learning environment and engaging climate for class participants.

2

Case Studies as Teaching Tools

Acase study to be used for teaching purposes is a narrative
description of a particular administrative or leadership problem or dilemma written from the point of view of one or more protagonists. Case studies with the greatest value and utility are
grounded in actual, institution-based administrative situations and
are almost always fact-based. The maxim that reality is stranger
than fiction is just as true in higher education as elsewhere, and the
greatest fodder for learning to struggle with issues in higher education can be found with greater richness in the real-life, day-to-day
administrative work being done on the nation's campuses than in
the imaginations of fiction writers. Well-written and thoroughly
researched cases, based on tough administrative problems facing colleges and universities, are powerful teaching tools.

Elements of an Effective Case Study

According to Wrage (1994), a good case shares a number of simi-
larities with a bad lecture. Good cases are ambiguous, full of conflict,
and leave important issues unresolved. Good cases are also complex,
and, in general, the more complex, the better. Complexity in a case
study ensures that issues will be open to multiple levels of analysis
(McNergney, Ducharme, and Ducharme, 1999) and that participants' perspectives will be varied and dynamic. Boehrer (1996) adds

that, in addition to being conflict-laden and complex, good cases introduce tension between alternative courses of action and end with more questions than answers.

In Robyn's (1986) opinion, cases with the greatest pedagogic utility are conflict-provoking and decision-forcing, and, while general enough for their lessons to apply to a myriad of situations, are also brief enough to sustain interest. She observes: "Any story contains elements that are unique as well as general, so developing a good case is often largely a matter of focus. The process can feel awkward, however, given the natural tendency of a writer-observer to adjust the lens for Halley's comet instead of the ever-present Milky-Way" (p. 4).

At their best, case studies on higher education issues present an administrative dilemma or problem in a way that captures the full complexity, dimensions, and difficulties of the actual real-life situations facing college and university leaders. The best cases present a clear chronology of events, highlight multiple viewpoints from a range of case "actors and actresses," and incorporate, when appropriate, original source materials (excerpts from memos, reports, and so on) that help capture the full reality of the situation. Cases also challenge teachers and students because they never provide as much information as one would like—one always wants to know more about what is happening and why. In this sense, cases mirror real-life decision-making situations where information is nearly always incomplete and time pressures are intense.

A good case is nonobvious; it presents participants with an interesting and challenging puzzle. In many instances, it describes a situation in which it is neither totally clear what the problem is nor what course of action decision makers should follow. Ideally, good case studies provide glimpses into the range of potentially conflicting perspectives and viewpoints that various constituents bring to a particular situation.

To a certain extent, effective ("good") cases and ineffective ("bad") cases are somewhat relative constructs. In one sense, an effective case might be defined as one that meets an instructor's pedagogical goals and facilitates learning. Conversely, an ineffective case might be defined as one that accomplishes neither of these tasks. In a more prescriptive sense, an effective case is likely to have at least a few of the following characteristics: 1) it is clearly written; 2) it has a well-laid out chronology; 3) it is focused on one or two core issues; 4) it has a compelling story line; 5) it addresses problems or dilemmas which are important to the field (in this case, of higher education); 6) it sustains discussion; 7) it presents a puzzle that lingers with participants long after case discussion is over; and 8) it links to broader problems of practice and a wider educational context.

Similarly, an ineffective case might have the following attributes: 1) its chronology and focus are vague, unclear, or confusing; 2) it presents a one-sided or skewed portrayal of events; 3) it lacks an obvious problem or dilemma; 4) it is too idiosyncratic and therefore inapplicable to other contexts; and 5) it fails to sustain readers' interest or participants' discussion.

Occasionally, an instructor will come across an exceptionally strong case that is particularly effective over a long period of time and for multiple audiences. A "classic" case is one that has at least a few of the following characteristics: 1) it focuses on a fundamental or core problem or dilemma that transcends time and institutional categories (such as evaluating academic programs or coping with constrained financial resources); 2) it is reflective of challenges and problems faced by a large number of institutions; 3) its story line is not only compelling but dramatic; and 4) it generates enthusiastic discussion. Students or institute participants who have worked through a classic case typically comment: "This could have been my institution;" "I saw myself in that case;" "That case will stick with me for quite some time."

It should be noted that some administrative situations lend

themselves quite easily to treatment in a case study. For example, issues involving particularly vexing leadership problems, innovative strategies for implementing new policies, or changes in institutional mission or priorities are all likely to present suitably complex and interesting dilemmas that could effectively be portrayed in a case study. Alternatively, situations involving nothing more than idiosyncratic personality clashes or the typical minutiae involved in daily decision making may not be broadly applicable to other institutional settings to make them worthwhile centerpieces for the development of a case study. The overarching topic or theme of an effective case study should be one faced by a broad enough array of institutional players in a range of administrative situations to make the case study both relevant and engaging for a variety of discussion participants.

Exercise: Which of the following scenarios would lend themselves well to treatment in a case study? Which scenario would be less suitable to the case study format? Why?

A small college has just completed a presidential search. Much to the faculty's surprise, the acting president, who is also the dean of the college, was not selected as the next president. Instead, the search committee selected an outsider with administrative experience at a large, urban research university. The case study focuses on the new president's challenges as he tries to assimilate into a new community and gain acceptance among some skeptical peers.

An assistant professor of history is dismissed for cause (based on extensive evidence and documentation) after regularly failing to show up for class, insubordination with colleagues and administrators, and fabricating publications to pad his resume. The case study focuses on the faculty member's personal recollections of his frus-

---

trations with his faculty colleagues and with the administrative
process that led to his termination.

The first example provides fodder for an interesting case study for
several reasons. First, the themes upon which it touches can be gen-
eralized and are familiar to many in the higher education field: leadership, transitions, campus politics, and a geographical clash of
campus cultures, to name but a few. Second, if well-written, this case
study should prove instructive to faculty members, presidents, search
committee members, and trustees, all of whom are impacted by leadership changes on campus and are familiar with the struggles that
accompany a newcomer who moves into a position of authority.
Third, while the case may center on a small college and a college
president, the issues can be broadly applied to many different campus environments (a women's college, master's institution, Big Ten
university) and many different leadership positions (a new provost,
department head, or board chair, for example). For these reasons, the
framework provided by the first scenario holds promise if developed
into a well-researched and well-written case study.

The second scenario, however, would be less likely to succeed as
an instructive case study. The issues it addresses, primarily an individual's anger and frustration with colleagues and administrative
policies, are almost too idiosyncratic in nature to prove useful to a
broader audience of graduate students or executive education program participants. In addition, since it appears that the reasons for
the dismissal are somewhat clear and supported by strong evidence,
the situation would lack a compelling dilemma upon which the case
would focus; a one-sided case discussion would be the likely result in
this instance. Finally, a case built solely upon an individual's anger
and frustration would probably not allow participants to take away
concrete lessons that would apply in broader institutional settings.

Selecting an Appropriate Case Study for a Higher Education Course or Professional Development Institute

The art of selecting the right case study, or series of cases, for a particular course or professional development institute depends on a number of factors:

- The course's or institute's broad themes and pedagogical goals

- The availability of thematically related topical and timely cases and related research

- Other items in the course's syllabus or on the institute's agenda

- The composition of the class, audience, or participant group

Some general course or institute themes—common critiques of higher education, for example—lend themselves quite easily to case study discussions because they are broad enough to make cases an appropriate and logical addition to the syllabus or institute curriculum. Other themes, such as technical changes in administrative computing systems, may have a smaller body of cases from which to draw, but those that are available may raise questions quite closely related to those posed in the course or institute.

Instructors who are inexperienced with case studies should start small. They would be well advised to incorporate only one or two cases into their courses or professional development program curricula. And they should certainly observe and learn from their peers who have had more experience integrating cases into their own courses.

The Harvard Institutes for Higher Education (HIHE) is a

leading source for case studies dealing with higher education administration.[1] HIHE regularly produces case studies on a wide range of policy and leadership topics, including governance, planning, academic administration, curriculum, and budgeting and resource allocation. Instructors interested in incorporating case studies into their teaching repertoire should also consult with faculty colleagues for pertinent cases, teaching notes (if available), and specific approaches for utilizing cases on various topics and issues.

Instructors should also consider other items on the syllabus when selecting a case or a mix of cases. A course with a tempered reading list may benefit from the addition of a particularly dramatic or controversial case study. On the other hand, a class that tends to erupt frequently into heated debates may gain from the inclusion of a case that raises underlying philosophical and theoretical questions relating to the problem or dilemma being discussed. For example, an instructor currently teaching a non-case-based course on budgeting and resource allocation in colleges and universities might consider including a case study that focuses on a particularly difficult and complex dilemma regarding budget cutbacks facing a university's senior leadership team. Such a case would not only be appropriate for and consistent with the course content but would also allow the instructor to link budgeting and resource allocation to other important topics such as leadership, governance, academic planning, and the like. If a teaching note were available, the instructor could gain specific insights on how best to utilize the case. Alternatively, the instructor might contact other faculty members who have used the case successfully in their classes.

1. To receive a current catalogue of HIHE case studies, contact Harvard Institutes for Higher Education, Harvard Graduate School of Education, 14 Story Street, 4th Floor, Cambridge, MA 02138.

Choosing Background Readings and Supporting Materials

Background readings can serve to situate the case's particular dilemma and details into a broader research and policy context. Case studies accompanied by pertinent, well-chosen supporting materials serve as a useful bridge between theory and practice. Before selecting background readings or supporting materials, instructors need to ask themselves what ideas and concepts they are trying to illuminate in the case discussion. For example, a Harvard case study about the University of Minnesota focuses on tenure reform, the power of anecdote and the media, the need for concrete data, and discord among board members and administrators.[2] To facilitate the link between theory and practice, theoretical, research-based readings on faculty tenure issues and governance and power in academic institutions would complement this particular case nicely and would constitute an excellent foundation and design for an effective case discussion session.

Once the instructor selects the cases and supporting materials, the real work begins. The art of teaching cases to students of higher education and higher education administrators and professionals requires a strategic mix of several ingredients: content knowledge, some professional or administrative experience, comfort with the case material, familiarity with case teaching methodology, and a willingness to set aside the traditional role of teacher in favor of what may be the less familiar role of guide and facilitator. Good case teaching takes practice and persistence; it is a craft that is learned over time. Improving one's case teaching skills is an ongoing process of learning from one's own experience and the experiences of other case teachers. It can be useful to watch other case teachers at work, to experiment and innovate, to practice and test, and to evaluate,

2. See Trower, Cathy. (2002) "University of Minnesota: The Politics of Tenure Reform." In James P. Honan and Cheryl Sternman Rule (eds.), *Casebook I: Faculty Employment Policies*. San Francisco: Jossey-Bass.

assess, and revise one's teaching techniques. It can also be helpful to have colleagues (other case teachers or teaching assistants) watch you and critique or comment on your style and effectiveness. Even videotaping one of your own case teaching sessions and debriefing with a more experienced instructor can prove enlightening. The important lesson here is to be comfortable but not complacent. As with all teaching, one's case teaching can always benefit from others' perspectives and input.

Essential Elements of
Effective Case Teaching

Just as familiarity with the various resource items on a syllabus—
be they print articles, Internet-based resources, films, or other
media—is a must for any competent, responsible instructor, so too
must case instructors be intimately familiar with the cases they plan
to utilize in class. This does not mean that case teachers need firsthand knowledge of the particular players, institutions, or administrative dilemmas presented in the cases (although such knowledge
can be quite helpful). Teaching notes prepared by case authors or
instructors who have taught the case before (and who also may
bring firsthand knowledge of the case and case context) are invaluable resources. See *Teaching Notes to Casebook I: Faculty Employment
Policies* (Jossey-Bass, 2002) for further information on this topic.

Before the Case Discussion Session

Before conducting a case discussion session, instructors will find it
useful to study all elements of a case, including the main issues,
dilemmas and conflicts, various personalities and players, and the
pros and cons of each key decision point in order to facilitate the
best possible discussion. Most instructors find it helpful to prepare
a written teaching plan that details the sequence of issues and topics to be covered. The teaching plan should include the major questions upon which the case discussion will focus. In a sense, this

document becomes the instructor's own version of a teaching note. Instructors can then modify and improve their "personal" teaching plan as they gain experience with a particular case.

Teaching Plan: The main elements of a teaching plan include the following:

- *Introduction.* A brief sentence or two introducing the case study and the institution upon which it is based.

- *Discussion themes.* The major themes and topics the case study will address. Some examples include the relationship between faculty salaries and productivity; the resistance department heads may face when instituting post-tenure reviews for the first time; or the dilemma of balancing an inclusive budgeting process with time and resource constraints.

- *Questions for participants.* Such questions can be given to participants in advance of the case study discussion for them to reflect upon while reading the case. Or they can be presented during the discussion itself. Or, as is generally the case, a little bit of both. Many veteran case instructors will offer one set of questions for advance reflection while reading and another set for in-class discussion. Examples of discussion questions include: What are the main elements of protagonist X's new policy? Do you agree with how she presented the policy to the faculty? Why or why not? What are the greatest challenges she faces if her policy is instituted?

- *Teaching tips.* These tips provide helpful advice to the instructor about how to maximize participation, improve time efficiency, and remain focused on the case's ultimate themes and goals. One helpful teaching tip is for an instructor to poll participants at the outset of a case discussion to assess their prior experience

---

with and knowledge of a particular topic. For example, when teaching a case study on strategic planning, the teaching tip may advise instructors to find out up front which students have participated in a strategic planning session before and in what capacity. He or she can then draw on these students as needed throughout the case discussion to find out whether their experiences meshed with the struggles and dilemmas faced by the protagonist and supporting players in the case.

- *Suggested activities.* These activities can run the gamut from dividing the participants into smaller groups to role-playing the protagonist to creating a set of policy alternatives to those presented in the case.

- *Wrap-up or take-aways.* The wrap-up section is where the instructor reviews the general themes of the case and asks participants to apply what they have learned to their own professional situations. In many senses, this is the most crucial part of the entire discussion, for it is where the instructor creates the bridge between the specific case and the "real life" of the students and participants who form the audience.

Planning in advance of a case session is crucial to ensuring a good discussion. Veteran case teachers also emphasize that the value of thorough preparation from both a content and process point of view simply cannot be overstated (Applegate, 1988).

To better illustrate the first two elements of a teaching plan—the introduction and discussion themes—we have provided a portion of a teaching plan for use with the Kansas State University case study.

Introduction

   Begin the session by exploring the growing interest in evaluating and assessing college and university faculty and, in particular, the growing interest in evaluating the work of tenured faculty. The work of Christine Licata and others (see Recommended Background Readings) can be referenced and described (frameworks for thinking about post-tenure review, range of policy examples and models, and comparative data on specific evaluation policies and procedures) as a way of putting the Kansas State case study into a broader national context. National data and statistics on the evaluation of tenured faculty might also be presented. Suggested discussion questions to guide participant preparation are also included at the end of this teaching note.

Discussion

   Plan to organize participant discussion of the Kansas State case around the following themes:

1. Problem identification, policy objectives, and policy context

2. Analysis of Kansas State Faculty evaluation policies

3. Assessment of policy outcomes and data needs for assessment

Clearly, introducing the case study and laying out the major themes to be covered are crucial first steps in any case discussion session.

Creating an Effective Classroom Setting for Case Teaching

The creation of an effective classroom setting for a case discussion will increase the likelihood of a productive teaching and learning experience for both the instructor and the case discussion participants. The classroom—or other discussion location—should be arranged in such a way as to ensure that participants can see and hear the instructor and one another. If the instructor finds himself or herself in a less than optimal instructional setting, the quality of the case discussion will clearly suffer. In large classrooms, the instructor may find it helpful to use a microphone. Some large classrooms are even equipped with microphones for students. Making use of these tools will enable all participants to benefit maximally from one another's contributions, particularly when the discussion group is large.

Materials That Support Effective Case Discussions

Name Cards

Providing name cards for all students greatly enhances the instructor's ability to maximize class participation and to weave together different threads of the conversation. Name cards also increase the likelihood that students will build on, or take issue with, the comments and observations of their peers, one of the primary goals of the discussion method of teaching. Name cards create a more personalized classroom environment and encourage continued interaction between the instructor and participants and among participants themselves after the class session concludes. Depending on the classroom configuration, it can be helpful for students to write their names on both sides of the name card. In this way, they can more easily identify one other, and the instructor can view the name cards from various vantage points in the classroom. The critical value in knowing one's audience will be discussed again later in this guidebook.

Chalkboards and Flipcharts

Learning to make effective use of the chalkboard or flipchart is a skill that any instructor will find invaluable, but for a case teacher, the benefits of possessing such a skill can be even more significant. Depending on the nature of the case they are teaching, instructors may choose to record on the chalkboard or flipchart, as part of their pre-class preparation, key facts or developments in a case that span a number of years. In other instances, instructors may prefer to wait until the discussion itself commences, calling on participants to provide the most important features of the case or the most crucial events in a case timeline or chronology.

Teaching Tip: When working with a strategic planning case, for example, instructors can present a timeline on the blackboard in a format as simple as this:

New president appointed: July 1999
Board of Trustees planning retreat: Sept. 1999
Campus planning meetings: Oct. 1999–Feb. 2000
Budget cuts announced by state legislature: March 2000
Revised strategic plan approved by Board: April 2000

Choices about whether, when, and how to use the blackboard or flipchart are largely matters of personal preference and will vary depending on the instructional goals of the case discussion and the composition of the participant group. But, if time is limited and the case is particularly complex, instructors and participants may benefit from seeing some of the case study's key elements displayed on the chalkboard or flipchart at the outset and diving right into the case's major themes. Such work can help the instructor "jump-start" a discussion and will minimize the likelihood that participants will get lost in factual and technical details. Because ongoing use of the chalkboard (or flipchart, whiteboard, and so on) provides participants with a visual representation and record of the case discussion as it unfolds, instructors might find it easier to make links among various ideas they have recorded. They can also refer back to comments and observations made earlier in the discussion.

Overhead Projector

Some case instructors and discussion leaders also find an overhead projector to be helpful, particularly where a case has numerous tables and exhibits whose interpretation will play a significant role in the case discussion. Displaying these exhibits during the discussion will improve the flow of the session by discouraging participants from burying their heads in their cases and flipping the pages to locate crucial facts or figures.

Other Pre-Session Teaching Tips

In addition to attending to some of the preparation techniques noted above, the instructor can take several other preliminary steps to ensure a productive case discussion session. Boehrer (1996), who has written numerous publications on the case study method, offers several pre-session teaching tips. Among them are:

- Place the case firmly within the framework of the course (or institute or workshop)

- Decide what supporting materials (background readings, relevant theory) to teach along with it

- Assign questions for the students to consider while they read the case in advance of the class discussion

- Formulate questions and likely responses in advance

- Think through multiple analyses

- Plan how to display students' responses

- Carefully consider how to close the case discussion

The following example presents a list of recommended background readings for use with the Kansas State University case:

Recommended Background Readings

Centra, John A. (1993). *Reflective Faculty Evaluation: Enhancing Teaching and Determining Faculty Effectiveness.* San Francisco: Jossey-Bass.

Chait, Richard P. (1998). "Post-Tenure Review of Department," in *Ideas in Incubation: Three Possible Modifications to Traditional Tenure Policies.* Washington, DC: American Association for Higher Education, pp. 13–20.

Goodman, Madeleine J. (1994) "The Review of Tenured Faculty at a Research University: Outcomes and Appraisals." *The Review of Higher Education 18*(1): 83–94.

Licata, Christine M., and Morreale, Joseph C. (1997). *Post-Tenure Review: Policies, Practices, Precautions.* New Pathways Working Paper Series, Inquiry #12, Washington, DC: American Association for Higher Education.

Seldin, Peter. (1990). *How Administrators Can Improve Teaching: Moving From Talk to Action in Higher Education.* San Francisco: Jossey-Bass.

Discussion Questions

Perhaps the most crucial of these advance tasks—one highlighted by Boehrer and several other authorities on case method instruction—is formulating pertinent, incisive, and compelling discussion questions (also sometimes referred to as "study questions"). A case instructor's skill at raising the "right" questions before and during a case discussion is a "cultivated art" (Wassermann, 1994, p. 76). Such questions "are the teacher's fundamental means of mediating the students' encounter with the material, guiding their exploration of it." (Boehrer, 1994, p. 15). No productive case session can proceed without carefully considered questions embedded in a coherent teaching strategy. Effective case discussion questions give participants a glimpse of the kinds of issues that the instructor might address and help point participants to the more important dilemmas and aspects of the case. Well-crafted discussion or study questions also provide links between the case and the participants' administrative practice by asking things like:

- What would you do in this situation?

- What advice would you offer the case protagonist?

- What might you have done differently?

- How do the lessons and insights from this case apply to your work as an administrator?

- Would the leadership approach taken by the protagonist in this case work for you? Why or why not?

These types of questions are intended to help participants connect the material presented in the case to their own leadership style and behaviors.

Consider a case that deals with the implementation of an innovative policy on faculty compensation. Effective discussion questions might include:

- What factors led to the development of the new policy in the first place?

- Did the new policy address expressed needs and policy objectives?

- Was the process by which the policy was developed a sound one?

- Did the implementation of the policy result in a good outcome for the institution?

These types of questions focus the students' attention on elements of the case the instructor will likely highlight during the case discussion.

To further illustrate the importance of discussion questions, consider these questions designed for use with the Kansas State University case:

Discussion Questions

1. Does the passage of Sections C31.5, C31.6, C31.7, and 31.8 adequately address the board of regents' concern about faculty performance and accountability? Why or why not?

2. Does the fact that Sections C31.5-C31.8 are implemented primarily on a departmental level make it more or less likely that potential faculty productivity problems will be identified and corrected?

3. Did the passage and implementation of Sections C31.5-C31.8 result in a good outcome at Kansas State? Why or why not?

4. What is your overall assessment of Kansas State's approach to organizational change? What elements of their change strategy are most significant to you? Why?

Anticipating Likely Responses

Formulating good discussion questions is only the beginning. For what good are the questions if the instructor is stymied by the replies? Equally important, then, is the instructor's ability to anticipate possible responses to these and other questions that participants may pose and to predict in which directions the discussion is likely to turn. Again, using the example of the case dealing with the implementation of an innovative faculty compensation system discussed earlier, an instructor could identify the various discussion pathways that the questions might follow in several ways. First, by predicting which case facts students would identify, the instructor could get a good sense of possible directions the discussion might take. The instructor should also anticipate both positive and negative comments about the policy itself and the process by which it was developed. If student responses tend toward either the positive or negative extreme, the instructor could then ask if anyone could make the case for the other side of the argument. The same would be true of the question concerning student perceptions about the outcome of the policy implementation. The instructor should anticipate and welcome multiple perspectives in crafting possible discussion pathways.

By mapping out potential discussion pathways in advance, instructors will be better prepared for their roles as facilitators and time managers and will more easily succeed in guiding the conversation back to the major themes of the case and, ultimately, the course. None of this is to suggest that case discussions are entirely predictable or that instructors should have inflexible "plans." Quite the contrary. The learning that takes place in a case discussion should be fresh and contain elements of unpredictability but should still focus on central ideas before the class session concludes. The best way to ensure that key learning points are raised is to attempt to anticipate the likely ebb and flow of the discussion beforehand.

Here is an example of a discussion question and likely responses as they relate to the Kansas State case:

What kinds of data would you want to collect on an ongoing basis to measure the impact of the new faculty evaluation policies at Kansas State?

Common responses to this question include: financial costs of implementing the new evaluation policies; trends regarding the number of faculty identified as chronic low-performers; trends regarding the number of complaints about faculty from students or parents to legislators and regents; instances of intrusion by regents in the future on faculty promotion and tenure decisions; analyses of improved learning outcomes among students; and examples of successful remediation.

Identifying Instructional Goals and Desired Learning Outcomes

Case instructors would be well-advised to accomplish one other essential task in advance of the case session itself: to establish instructional goals for the case discussion. The fundamental questions for the instructor to address are: Why am I teaching this case? What concepts or ideas am I trying to get across to participants? What do I want participants to learn from this case? Part of the task of setting instructional goals is having some idea of how the case discussion might begin and end. One way to think about this issue is to pose the questions: Where do I want participants to be at the end of this case discussion? What do I want them to take away from the discussion? Thinking about the answers to these questions in advance of the session can provide the instructor with valuable insights into how to structure and design the case discussion.

For example, an instructor teaching a case study on the leader's role in institutional transformation might identify several key learning points or take-aways they would like the case discussion to revolve around. If the desired learning points of the session were: leaders need to articulate a clear institutional vision, transformation efforts should be linked to governance and resource allocation processes, and transformation efforts should be constantly monitored by leaders, then the instructor should craft a teaching plan that highlights how these issues are illustrated in the case study. By spending time in the case discussion focusing on elements of the desired learning outcomes, the instructor increases the likelihood that discussion participants will see the relevance of learning points and take-aways and will be able to link ideas from the case discussion to broader themes and frameworks and to their own administrative practice.

Following are some instructional goals for teaching the Kansas State case:

- To examine factors that trigger campus discussions and policy deliberations concerning faculty evaluation

- To analyze the processes through which faculty evaluation policies are discussed, deliberated, and developed

- To identify ways to assess the effectiveness and outcomes of faculty evaluation procedures

- To identify data elements that would assist in this assessment

---

During the Case Discussion Session

Know Your Audience

One of the most important hurdles any case instructor must surmount is turning a group of stranger-observers into a group of active participants in their own learning and in the learning of others. It is crucial, then, for a case instructor to get to know his or her audience. Name cards, as noted earlier, are a useful first step, but they reveal little about a person's background or experience.

In a course that spans several weeks or months, instructors will have ample time to gain a sense of their students' backgrounds, prior professional experience in higher education, and possible stance on particularly sensitive issues. However, those who teach in short-term or single-session executive or professional education programs are less likely to have such background knowledge before the session actually begins. The investment of a few minutes' time for introductions at the outset of the session will make for a more valuable and productive experience for teacher and participant alike. The instructor can use this knowledge of participants' positions, backgrounds, and interests to draw them more fully into the discussion and help contextualize their viewpoints on the case. For example, when teaching a case study on shared governance, it would be helpful for all in the room to know who are faculty members, administrators, and trustees, and who hails from large or small, and public or private institutions. Of course, depending on the size of the group, obtaining such information in the allotted time frame may be difficult or, perhaps, unrealistic, but making an effort to do so before conducting the session is generally worthwhile for both the instructor and the participants.

Experience Level and Composition of the Group

The instructor should have a good grasp of what the experience level and composition of the participant group will be. Needless to say, a group of beginning graduate students in higher education administration with little or no prior administrative experience will bring a different set of perspectives and viewpoints to a case discussion than will a group of experienced deans, department chairs, and senior administrators.

A brief poll at the beginning of a case discussion session can be a very effective means for doing a general assessment of the overall experience level and knowledge base of the participant group. For example, the instructor of a case focusing on budget issues might ask, "How many people are familiar with the different types of budget techniques and formats?" or "How many individuals have had direct experience managing a grant budget?" The answers to these questions provide the instructor with immediate and valuable information on how to best conduct the case discussion for a particular group. In some instances, lack of prior knowledge and experience with the issues highlighted in the case study might signal the need for the instructor to do a brief "mini-lecture" highlighting key concepts and ideas before moving into the case discussion itself.

After assessing the experience level of the participant group, instructors would be well-advised to adjust their teaching plans accordingly. If the group consists of individuals who all hold the same position (deans, trustees, faculty members, and so on), the instructor might want to incorporate some discussion of the likely perspectives of individuals in roles other than the ones held by the participants. In other words, a participant group of trustees would do well to ponder, "How might the faculty handle this issue?" The general principle here is for the instructor to be aware of the experience levels and professional backgrounds of the participant group and to incorporate this knowledge into the discussion plan. Teaching notes for specific cases frequently include potential strategies for accomplishing this.

Timing Issues

Frequency and Duration of Contact

One factor deserving the case instructor's attention and consideration is the frequency and duration of contact he or she will have with the group. A "one-shot" case discussion with a new audience and no planned follow-up is quite different from a fifteen-session weekly course using cases. Indeed, perhaps the most difficult assignment for a case instructor is the "one-shot" case session. In this situation, the instructor usually has limited information about the participants and only a single opportunity to engage them in the case discussion. The lack of opportunity for follow-up or mid-course correction can pose significant, but not insurmountable, challenges for the instructor.

Take as an example a three-hour "one-shot" case discussion session with department chairs which will focus on a brief case study dealing with declining enrollment in a music department. In such a session, assuming that participants have had little or no time for prior preparation for the discussion, the instructor might use the following format:

1. Brief introductions, followed by sufficient time to review and read the case study (assuming preparation level is somewhat mixed).

2. Participants engage in brief small group (two to three individuals) discussions of the case and discussion questions. This will help participants establish connections with one another and with the case material.

3. After a short break, the instructor is then in a position to engage the entire group in a discussion of the various issues in the case, such as program discontinuance, or the reassignment or dismissal of members of the music faculty.

Since instructors and participants in a "one-shot" case session have little or no opportunity for reflection on or continued discussion of the case and the issues it raises, the above approach attempts to maximize existing learning opportunities given these constraints.

Alternatively, instructors and participants who have multiple opportunities to interact with the case material and one another can revisit, reflect on, and perhaps continue discussion of particular aspects of the case in subsequent sessions.

Time Management

The case instructor is also responsible for keeping a close eye on the clock. Here is where formulating instructional goals and a solid teaching plan in advance of the discussion truly pays off. The pace and flow of a case session depend, in large part, on the instructor's ability to ensure that major themes are identified and explored with ample time for analysis and reflection. A stimulating case discussion can sometimes raise passions, which, once expressed, can often turn a tame classroom into a hotbed of activity. While such an atmosphere is one many instructors strive to create, it is nonetheless essential that the conversation remain on course and that the instructor maintain the group's focus on key issues. Should the discussion move off-track, the instructor will want to take charge and refocus the questions. Comments such as "That's a good point, but let's hold off on that issue for a few minutes" will help participants feel valued but enable the instructor to retain control over the direction of the discussion. (Returning to the participant's comment at a later point, if time allows, is certainly important.) Appropriate pacing is also essential. Should the discussion get bogged down, saying "We need to move on," or "one more comment on this issue, then I want to ask you another question" is vital toward moving the discussion along and meeting all of the teaching goals for the session.

> *Teaching Tip:* As part of a time management plan for the case discussion session, the instructor might also consider engaging participants in different types of interactions (large group, small group, dyads/triads, role plays, and so on) as a way of varying the pace of the session and breaking up the overall flow of the discussion into discrete segments.

Effective time management, appropriate pacing, and a smooth flow based on a well-formulated teaching plan can all assist in meeting these goals.

Case Discussion Techniques, Applications, and Strategies

In its most basic form, a case discussion involves an instructor in focused dialogue and conversation with a group of participants. A number of techniques and strategies can, when used appropriately, enhance this type of discussion teaching and provide participants with additional opportunities for vivid and powerful learning. Depending on the instructor's skill level and instructional goals, the nature of the case study, and the composition of the participant group, one or more of these techniques can be used in the course of a discussion.

Role Playing or Simulation

Some case studies, because they describe the actions, perspectives, and roles of various case actors, lend themselves to the use of role-playing or simulation techniques. For example, in a case that focuses on governance issues and provides sufficient background information on what the president and trustees are thinking and doing, the instructor might ask one participant to play the role of the president and another to play a trustee. These participants can then engage in a brief dialogue that mirrors an actual decision option or possible policy solution in the case. By modeling what a conversation between two case actors might actually sound like, the instructor can give participants a firsthand glimpse into difficult problems of administrative practice and how they might be addressed.

Another way to highlight the various goals, interests, and aspirations of various constituents in a case is to divide the participants into constituent groups (trustees, provosts, faculty, students, and so on) and ask them to identify that group's goals and points of view in the case under discussion. The technique can help participants better appreciate and grapple with, firsthand, the various perspectives each group brings to the case dilemma or problem.

Following is an example of a role-playing activity for use with the Kansas State Case:

Activity: If the instructor so chooses, a discussion-facilitating exercise may be used at this point. Divide participants into three role-play groups: regents, provost, and faculty. Organize the role play discussion as follows:

Regents group: What do you hope to accomplish with this mandate? What are your policy objectives?

Provost group: In light of the regents' mandate, what do you hope to achieve?

Faculty group: What do you do now that this issue is on your plate? Is the regents' request reasonable? Should the faculty resist?

An overarching question that can be posed to all three groups is: What pitfalls must you work to avoid?

Protagonist Visit

In some instances (especially when the instructor has firsthand knowledge of the case site and direct access to case actors), the instructor might want to invite the actual case protagonist to take part in the class (either in person or via audio-conference or video-conference). This strategy provides participants with a potentially powerful and vivid opportunity to get a firsthand account of a particular case situation. As with other applications and strategies, instructors should build the inclusion of a case protagonist into their overall teaching plan and do some advance thinking about how an actual case protagonist can most productively be incorporated into a case discussion.

Two approaches for including the case protagonist in case discussion sessions have proven to be effective: (1) The instructor can invite the case protagonist to sit in for the entire case discussion and to offer commentary and take questions from students. When using this approach, the instructor should introduce the protagonist at the beginning of the session and note to the group that he or she will listen to the case discussion and take part in the class during the final fifteen or twenty minutes. In some instances, it is possible that the presence of the case protagonist might inhibit discussion of a case, but this has not been our general experience. (2) Alternatively, the instructor can arrange for the case protagonist to take part in a portion of the case discussion session (a key decision point, update of the case situation, and so on) via audio-conference or video-conference. When using this approach, the instructor can either alert participants in advance to the fact that the case protagonist will take part in a portion of the discussion or include the case protagonist via audio or video unannounced in advance (both approaches have pros and cons). In either instance, it is help-ful for the instructor to take the first few minutes of the audio or video link to briefly summarize for the case protagonist the key points raised in the case discussion (since he or she did not take part in this portion of the session). This will allow for a somewhat "seamless" flow from the case discussion to the audio or video update or question and answer session with the case protagonist.

A protagonist visit can be used to many different ends in addi-tion to reacting to participants' comments and answering questions. Protagonists can update participants on the current situation that the case has addressed on campus, describe what he or she would have done differently (if anything) had circumstances been differ-ent or had more information been available at the time, describe what will happen next on campus, and the like. Students and par-ticipants not only find the ability to interact directly with case pro-tagonists to be informative, but they also find it exciting. Like actors on-screen or in a play, case protagonists become somewhat larger than life due to the intensity of many case discussions. Many par-ticipants feel they get to know these protagonists by absorbing the details presented in the cases. Being able to ask them questions directly is a real treat; it heightens the excitement in the classroom and adds a new dimension to the entire case learning experience.

Dyads and Triads

Case discussions do not always need to involve the entire partici-pant group in conversation with the instructor. It can be helpful to provide opportunities for participants to discuss particular issues, topics, and questions in groups of two or three. These types of con-versations should be built into the instructor's overall teaching plan. For example, if the instructor is interested in having participants develop alternative courses of action for a case protagonist, he or she can ask participants to talk with one or two of their colleagues for a brief period (five to fifteen minutes depending on the instructor's plan and goals) about what they would do if they were in the protagonist's shoes. Following these brief conversations, the instructor can reconvene the entire participant group and continue the discussion with the group as a whole.

Monitoring and Encouraging Participation in Case Discussions

The best case discussions allow for all voices to be heard. Instructors need to be constantly aware of who is participating and who is not. It may be helpful to state at the start of the case session that good discussions require broad participation. As much of the power of case learning comes from the comments and observations of participants, instructors should take responsibility for creating the conditions under which all participants feel comfortable expressing their thoughts and ideas. If participation is somewhat mixed or is dominated by a few individuals, the instructor can ask, "Is there anyone whom we have not yet heard from?" or "Can anyone offer a perspective on this issue that we have not yet heard?" These and other efforts to encourage discussion signal that the instructor seeks broad and sustained participation.

As noted earlier, it can also be helpful, if time and logistics permit, to talk with students or participants outside of the classroom or institute setting to get a sense of their interests and experience and to encourage them to play an active role in the case discussion. For example, Harvey, a student who was not active in case discussions, noted in one postclass conversation with the instructor, that the institution described in the most recent case was very similar to an institution where he previously worked. The instructor can use this information to call on Harvey at the opening of the next class and have him share his personal experiences of working at an institution like the one the students had studied together during the prior case session. The instructor's added effort in situations like this will encourage all students, even those who may have difficulty diving into an open discussion, to share their viewpoints and experiences.

Ideally, the discussion of a case will be a learning space within which all participants can feel comfortable and empowered to test ideas and views that "real world" administrative settings do not always permit. Students and participants should be reminded frequently that case sessions are "safe spaces" where the opportunity to try out and test solutions and strategies does not have the negative consequences of proposing politically or financially costly solutions in actual institutional settings. So while the negative consequences of proposing an unpopular strategy are minimal (at worst, strongly voiced disagreement from classmates), the positive aspects—thinking up a novel solution to a persistent problem and receiving positive feedback from classroom or institute peers—can be quite rewarding. Of course, the greatest reward would be bringing the new ideas back to one's institutional setting having already tested them out among a group of professional peers.

Providing Balance

In some situations, even if broad participation is taking place, the discussion might be particularly one-sided. For example, perhaps everyone in the group appears to be saying that an administrator in a particular case is doing a good job working with the board of trustees. In this instance, the instructor might play devil's advocate and ask: "Is there anyone who thinks the administrator is not doing a good job working with the board?" or "Could anyone make an argument that the administrator is not doing a good job working with the trustees?" Efforts such as these can serve to add balance to a lopsided case discussion and can help to ensure that multiple perspectives and points of view are uncovered and articulated. It is important to note that a good case discussion does not necessarily result in consensus among participants. In fact, the instructor should encourage participants to articulate as many viewpoints as possible in a case discussion. Rather than trying to "crack the case" or come up with the "right" or "perfect" solution, the case discussion participants should attempt to see and appreciate many points of view and possible solutions to a particular case problem or dilemma.

The following examples of further questions in the Kansas State case illustrate how to get participants to broaden their thinking:

- With regard to the regents' mandate, why aren't the regents concerned about identifying and rewarding high achievers rather than focusing on chronic low performers?

- Should chronic low performers on campus, faculty *and* administrators, be identified internally?

- Under Kansas State's newly established faculty evaluation policies, could we discover, if we wanted to, who the chronic low performing faculty are?

- Was the provost wise to immediately delegate the issue to the faculty senate?

- What is your assessment of the context within which discussions of faculty evaluation policies at Kansas State were taking place?

- Was it a good time for such discussions to be taking place? Why or why not?

- To what extent was the campus prepared or not prepared for such policy deliberations?

Fleshing Out the Big Ideas

Case instructors must attempt to balance two somewhat different broad instructional goals: 1) to systematically analyze the case itself, and 2) to link the case to the broader policy context and to relevant research findings, theories, and analytic frameworks. During the course of good case discussions, the instructors will address both the particulars of a case (case facts, main players, institutional characteristics, possible action steps, and so on) and the big ideas of a course (concepts and findings from the research literature, theories, analytic frameworks, and so on). As noted above, the instructor's pairing of case studies with appropriate readings will make this link more explicit for participants. Instructors can also play a significant role in linking the case to the broader policy context and to research and theory by integrating insightful questions into the case discussion. The following questions may be helpful:

- To what extent do the particulars of this case illustrate challenges or dilemmas in the larger world of administrative practice in higher education? What is similar? What is different?

- To what extent does the case illustrate the theory or analytic framework? How does one account for the misalignment of theory and practice?

Instructors should also attempt to broaden the ideas and insights from a particular case context to the larger context of various institutional settings. To achieve this, the instructor might pose questions such as: What if the institution we focused on in the case discussion had been public instead of private? A large research university instead of a small liberal arts college? Questions such as these make it possible to "translate" case lessons across institutional types and boundaries.

Similarly, the instructor can also attempt to place the particular case under consideration into context in relation to other institutional examples. For example, a particular case about cost containment in administrative units might be quite typical and reflective of common and general practices among many institutions. Conversely, a case about a particularly innovative approach to faculty development might be somewhat more unique and atypical. In both instances, the instructor should attempt to show how the particular case "fits" in relation to other institutional examples of this particular policy dilemma or problem highlighted in the case.

Closing the Case Discussion Session

Just as it is important for the instructor to have a good teaching plan and to think about how to open a case discussion and sustain participation, it is also important to provide an effective closing to the case discussion. There are a number of strategies for "ending well." For example, the instructor can signal to the group that time remains for only one or two final comments. After this signal has been offered and the final comments have been made, the instructor can provide the participants with some brief summary comments or learning points to illustrate key insights from the discussion.

Alternatively, the instructor may want to invite participants to offer their own learning points or take-aways. In this approach, the instructor can take a few minutes at the end of the session to pose questions such as: What are the key lessons or insights that you take away from this case discussion? What sense do you make of the major challenges and dilemmas we have discussed? The important insight here is to give some prior thought to how best to end the case discussion in a way that maximizes and captures the essential learning that has taken place.

Examples of take-aways from the Kansas State case include:

---

1. It is important to be aware of the impetus for policy discussions of faculty employment issues. In this case, the regents' mandate for revising faculty development policies triggered the events in the case, and meeting the requirements of this mandate was reflected in the policies that were ultimately created. Policy discussions at other institutions might be convened in response to other triggers (such as legislatures, presidents, or provosts) and result in alternative outcomes; it is important to understand such differences.

2. Leadership style, governance issues, and process are important ingredients for effective policy deliberations concerning faculty employment policies. In this case, the fact that there was stable

leadership at the institution and that there had been prior campus conversations concerning faculty evaluation policies through existing governance structures made it possible for sustained policy deliberations to take place and for subsequent policy implementation. These factors are important to the overall understanding of reviewing and revising faculty employment policies.

4

Post-Discussion Learning

Opportunities and Challenges

After the case discussion has ended, the instructor has the potential to create a bridge from the case discussion to a number of post-discussion learning opportunities. Among the questions the instructor should ask himself or herself are: What are the participants taking away from the case discussion? What sense and meaning do they make of the case discussion in terms of its application to their own administrative practice? In many instances, the best case discussions are those that stick with the participants (and the instructor) well after the session concludes. As Boehrer (1996) observes, "a good case discussion tends to transcend the case itself" (p. 4). Ideally, a productive and thoughtful case discussion is more than the sum of its parts.

Applications to Administrative Practice

Case studies and case discussions should be viewed as means to fundamental ends. They represent powerful metaphors that can link the experiences of others with one's own actions and behaviors. At its best, case learning should have some connection and applicability to one's work and practice. Learners can benefit from case-based courses insofar as they succeed in drawing lessons and insights from the case discussion and can apply these lessons to their own professional experience. This type of learning can have two dimensions: one that makes comparisons to one's own situation and perhaps affirms or clarifies one's own actions and efforts, and another that highlights differences between what occurred in the case (and case discussion) and one's own administrative actions and behaviors. The instructor should be mindful of the potential benefit of both forms of case learning.

Reservations and Caveats

Pitfalls to Avoid

No pedagogical approach is above criticism or limitations, and case teaching is no exception. While this guide seeks to provide advice and insights for instructors to maximize the use and benefits of this particular approach to teaching, it is important to acknowledge that not all cases are good teaching tools and not all case discussions are productive learning experiences. A poorly written or badly conceived case study can be an enormous obstacle to a good learning experience. A case in which there is no compelling dilemma or problem nor a variety of disparate points of view will undoubtedly lead to a somewhat flat and lifeless discussion. Instructors should be mindful of their own sense of what a good case study looks like—in many instances, this is a trial and error process that comes with experience. Over time, knowing a "good" case becomes intuitive and second nature.

Similarly, a haphazardly planned session for which the instructor did not adequately prepare is equally problematic. To the greatest extent possible, instructors should be clear as to why they are teaching a case in the first place and what type of learning experience they are trying to create. Without this type of reflection, a case discussion is nothing more than an interesting chat with little or no substantive value to participants. Case teaching represents just one of a number of pedagogical tools and approaches from which instructors can choose. In some instructional settings, it might not be the right tool for the job; instructors should be mindful of this possibility and always consider the use of other pedagogical approaches if they are more appropriate.

It is also important to note the criticisms of the case method of teaching that various scholars have raised. For example, Argyris's (1980) critique of the case method details a number of reservations about the ultimate value of case teaching. He suggests that the case method inhibits "double-loop learning." In other words, parsing a case and discussing various courses of action may fall short of compelling students to question why certain decisions were made and may not do enough to influence their own decision-making process in the future. For example, if an instructor has engaged participants in an extensive discussion of various potential courses of action in a particular administrative situation, he or she might then spend some time focusing on the rationale for a particular decision (either the decision actually made or the various decision options that have been posited in the discussion). The question the instructor might pose here is: Why did the case protagonist do X? (in the actual situation) or Why should the protagonist have done Y? (in the various hypothetical courses of action posed).

Another approach to better approximate the "double-loop learning" described by Argyris involves advising case discussion participants to explicitly consider how the lessons and insights from the case study and the case discussion do or do not apply to their own professional and administrative experiences. Such efforts encourage participants to think beyond the parameters of the case discussion itself to a broader policy context and to additional applications of the case's lessons to one's own administrative practice. Instructors should continue to be mindful of the limitations and criticisms of case teaching and to make efforts to address concerns about this pedagogical approach and its use.

Final Thoughts

This guide and the teaching notes that accompany individual case studies are intended to provide potential instructors and discussion leaders with a basis and starting point for effective case teaching. It is important to note that such resources represent just that—a

starting point. The ideas and suggestions we have presented should
be adapted to the instructor's needs and style, to the particular composition of the participant group, to the topic of the case being
taught, and to the instructional goals of the discussion itself. The
real work of case teaching is not in the planning and preparation,
although they are both important. The real work is in the doing, in
actually convening the case discussion and working with the comments, observations, and views of real discussion participants. Good
case teachers practice a lot and learn from their experiences. As
with other skills and arts, the willingness to continue to practice
and to learn is essential. When done well, case teaching has the
potential to change the way people think about themselves and
their work as administrators and managers. Instructors might also
find themselves thinking about their own teaching in new ways.

Roland Christensen (1991, in Barnes, Christensen, and Hansen,
1994) summed up the power and impact of discussion teaching on
the teaching and learning process perhaps better than anyone else
in the field:

> The most fundamental observation about discussion
> teaching I can make is this: however mysterious or elu-
> sive the process may seem, it can be learned. Through
> collaboration and cooperation with friends and col-
> leagues, and through self-observation and reflection,
> teachers can master both principles and techniques of
> discussion leadership. But the task is complex. Discus-
> sion teachers' responsibilities are as varied as their
> rewards. With greater vitality in the classroom, the sat-
> isfaction of true intellectual collaboration and synergy,
> and improved retention on the part of students, the
> rewards are considerable. The responsibilities may be dif-
> ficult to appreciate at first. For example, effective prepa-
> ration for discussion classes takes more time, because
> instructors must consider not only *what* they will teach,

but also *who* and *how*. And the classroom encounter con-
sumes a great deal of energy; simultaneous attention to
process (the flow of activities that make up a discussion)
and content (the material discussed) requires emotional
as well as intellectual engagement. Effective discussion
leadership requires competency in both areas; it can only
be achieved with patience [p. 23].

In our view, good case teaching can yield significant benefits for
both instructors and students. At its best, case teaching engages
teachers and learners in focused dialogues on pressing problems of
practice. At a time when we are expecting more of our leaders and
managers in higher education, case teaching and learning can make
a powerful contribution to the problem-solving skills of those
charged with running our colleges and universities.

Annotated Bibliography

Applegate, Lynda. (1988). "Case Teaching at Harvard Business School: Some Advice for New Faculty." President and Fellows of Harvard College. Harvard Business School Case No. 9-189-062.

This note grounds newcomers to case teaching methodology in the fundamentals, including the value of thorough preparation, the role of the instructor in relation to the student, and the importance of process as well as content.

Argyris, Chris. (1980). "Some Limitations of the Case Method: Experiences in a Management Development Program." *Academy of Management Review,* 5(2): 291–298.

This article provides a critical analysis of the case method as applied to executive education programs. It notes both descriptive features of case method teaching and learning and highlights shortcomings and potential pitfalls.

Barnes, Louis B., C. Roland Christensen, and Abby J. Hansen. (1994). *Teaching and the Case Method.* (3rd ed.) Boston: Harvard Business School Press.

One of the definitive volumes on the subject of case teaching, this volume uses essays and numerous actual cases to provide an overview to the field of case teaching and discussion-based pedagogy.

Boehrer, John. Undated. "Learning with Cases." Adapted from an orientation message on case learning prepared for students at Saint Olaf College by Professor David Schodt.

This brief discussion geared towards students summarizes what a case is and provides suggestions for preparing case studies and discussing them in class.

Boehrer, John. "Case Learning: How Does It Work? Why Is It Effective?" Based on *Questions and Answers About Case Learning*, adapted by Thomas Angelo and John Boehrer at the Kennedy School of Government from an article of the same title by Thomas Bonoma of Harvard Business School.

This brief summary outlines the benefits and advantages of case method teaching and learning.

Boehrer, John. (1994). "On Teaching a Case." *International Studies Notes*, 19(2): 14–20.

Offering some general guidance on case teaching, Boehrer highlights the importance of understanding the case material, the case teaching process, and the larger role cases play in the teaching-learning enterprise. He emphasizes the need for case instructors to ask good questions and outlines the various steps involved in leading an effective case discussion.

Boehrer, John. (1996). "How to Teach a Case." Kennedy School of Government Case Program, no. N18-95-1285.0. © 1995 by the President and Fellows of Harvard College, © 1996 by the Cascade Center for Public Service.

This note presents a schematic rendering of a lecture versus a case discussion, describes the nature of a case discussion, provides tips on case teaching and preparation, and reflects on the costs and benefits of case method pedagogy.

Boehrer, John, and M. Linsky. (1990). "Case Discussion: What Is It Like? What Is Its Purpose?" Excerpted from "Teaching with Cases:

Learning to Question." In M. D. Svinicki (ed.), *The Changing Face of College Teaching*. New Directions for Teaching and Learning, no. 42. San Francisco: Jossey-Bass.

Similar to Boehrer's other pieces, this particular one-page piece also contrasts case learning with traditional classroom learning. The page ends by highlighting eight main purposes of a case discussion.

Hammond, John S. (1980). (Based on earlier notes by E. Raymond Corey and Martin Marshall.) "Learning by the Case Method." The President and Fellows of Harvard College, Harvard Business School Case no. 9-376-241.

This note is geared to participants in case study discussions and describes the educational purposes of a case, tips on preparing for a case-based class, and what to expect during a case discussion.

McDade, Sharon. (1988). "An Introduction to the Case Study Method: Preparation, Analysis, and Participation." President and Fellows of Harvard College.

This note provides a concise description of the basic components of a case study and its uses as a pedagogical tool and places special emphasis on the value of instructor preparation and class participation. It includes nine suggested pointers to follow when analyzing case studies and a list of additional bibliographic references.

McNergney, Robert F., Edward R. Ducharme, and Mary K. Ducharme (eds.). (1999). "Teaching Democracy Through Cases." In *Educating for Democracy: Case Method Teaching and Learning*. Mahwah, NJ: Erlbaum.

This philosophical account of the role of cases in teaching students about democracy makes a useful point about the value of complexity in cases.

Merseth, Katherine K. (1998). "Cases, Case Methods, and the Professional Development of Educators." ERIC Clearinghouse on Teaching and Teacher Education.

This piece defines cases and case methods, describes how and when to use case studies, and explores future uses of case studies in teacher education.

Nelson, Marianne T. (1996, September). Teaching with Cases: Instructional Methods (A Literature Review). Qualifying Paper Submitted by Marianne T. Nelson, Harvard Graduate School of Education.

This comprehensive, amply cited account of a broad spectrum of case teaching literature covers a variety of topics, from the historical roots of the case method to the elements of an effective case discussion to the role of multimedia instructional cases. It also contains an extensive bibliography and an annotated matrix of case teaching methods.

Robyn, Dorothy. (1986). "What Makes a Good Case?" Kennedy School of Government Case Program, no. N15-86-673.0.

The five essential elements of a good teaching case are presented in this note.

Swamidass, Paul. (October, 1998). "How To Get the Most Out of Cases." Distributed by Harvard Business School Case Services, no. 9-381-668.

While focused largely on management and business cases, this note underscores the advantages of case teaching more generally.

Using Technology: Bolstering Case Discussion in Teaching Materials (Harvard Business School Publications)

This newsletter article describes how faculty members at the Harvard Business School use the Internet to have students submit responses to case questions before class. The professors then analyze these responses and use them to tailor class discussions.

Wassermann, Selma. (1994). *Introduction to Case Method Teaching.* New York: Teachers College Press.

Wassermann's comprehensive book is dedicated to all aspects of the case teaching process. While focusing largely on secondary school teachers and issues, it contains sufficiently broad information to make it more generally applicable as well.

Welty, William M. (1989). "Discussion Method Teaching: How to Make It Work." *Change*, July/August, 41–49.

This article addresses the value of discussion-based teaching and contains sections on pre-class preparation, the teaching environment, the elements of a teaching session, and post-session ideas. It also includes a valuable text box entitled "Resources for Further Help."

Wrage, Stephen. (1994, Spring). "Best Case Analysis: What Makes a Good Case and Where to Find the One You Need." *International Studies Notes*, 19(2) 21–27.

This article, designed for both the novice and experienced case teacher, presents the results of a survey of recipients of Pew Faculty Fellowships. Respondents commented on the definition of a case, the elements of a good case, and the best types of cases for different purposes and class subjects. The article ends with a source and address list from which more information (and specific cases) can be obtained.

Appendix

Kansas State University Case Study
Evaluating and Addressing Chronic Low Achievement

Holly Madsen

When Provost James Coffman received a list of seven recommendations regarding faculty evaluation from the Kansas
Board of Regents in March 1995, the message was clear: "The board
expects [the recommendations] to be implemented in this important area of accountability to our public" (see Exhibit 1 at the end
of the chapter). The sensitive issues addressed in the memo grew,
in part, out of the board's reaction to public complaints about higher
education generally, and a rising clamor over faculty accountability
more particularly. As John Welsh, Executive Director of the Board
of Regents, explained, "Over the years, some faculty members have
been dismissed over low performance, and the regents saw these
cases drag out over time in the media. They wanted to empower

Holly Madsen prepared this case under the supervision of Richard P. Chait, professor of higher education, Harvard Graduate School of Education, as the basis for
class discussion rather than to illustrate either effective or ineffective handling of
an administrative situation.

This case was prepared for the Project on Faculty Appointments and
funded by the Pew Charitable Trusts. © 1998 by the President and Fellows of Harvard College. No part of this publication may be reproduced, stored in a retrieval
system, used in a spreadsheet, or transmitted in any form or by any means—electronic, mechanical, photocopying, recording, or otherwise—without the permission of the Project on Faculty Appointments at the Harvard Graduate School of
Education.

K-State and the other university administrators to do something about it." The head of the Department of Philosophy, James Hamilton, said, "The regents were reacting to the legislature, which gets phone calls from parents. They are reacting to the broad perception that professors don't work very hard."

The recommendations called for regular evaluations of faculty members by multiple parties, specifying that the university should use "instruments to measure student rating of instruction [that] solicit, at a minimum, student perspectives on (a) the delivery of instruction; (b) the assessment of learning; (c) the availability of the faculty members to students; and (d) whether the goals and objectives of the course were met." The board also directed the university to develop a goal-setting process and regularly engage department heads in the evaluation of individuals.

In addition, the regents directed department chairs to clearly "allocate the amount of effort the faculty member will devote to teaching, research, and service" based on institutional and departmental goals. The board noted, "merit evaluation of faculty should follow this agreement." Most contentious among the regents' recommendations was the call for a new policy on "chronic low performance." Section 7a of Exhibit 1 reads: "Each campus should i) provide assistance for faculty renewal and development, ii) define chronic low performance, and iii) examine dismissal policies to include chronic low performance, *despite all assistance*, as an indicator of incompetence."

It was the latter recommendation, in particular, that set in motion a process of spirited negotiations between and among faculty leaders and administrators culminating in a new university policy intended to identify and address "chronic low achievement."

Kansas State University

Set in the rolling Flint Hills of northeast Kansas, Kansas State University sprawls over a 664-acre campus in the town of Manhattan,

125 miles west of Kansas City. Known as K-State, the university was founded in 1863 as a land-grant institution under the Morrill Act. In 1997–98, K-State enrolled 20,300 students and employed 1,600 faculty members (including graduate assistants), of whom 900 were tenured. In recent years, the university has placed particular emphasis on the synthesis of scholarship and teaching. In 1997, K-State was one of ten research institutions in the nation to receive a National Science Foundation award recognizing its work in integrating research and education in the sciences.

The Kansas Board of Regents is a nine-member body that oversees K-State and five other state universities, including the University of Kansas. Members are appointed by the governor and confirmed by the Kansas Senate.

Creating a Context for Collaboration

On a humid spring day in his office in Anderson Hall, Dr. Coffman, who had been provost for eleven years, reflected on the series of events spurred by the regents' mandate.

From the outset of his term as provost, Coffman set the tone for collaborative and cooperative work with the faculty—an approach followed at K-State since the beginning of President Jon Wefald's administration in 1986. "The process was advanced a few years ago, in some ways, when the vice president for administration and finance, the legislative liaison, and I visited every college of the university to discuss the legislative budget for the university," Coffman recalled. State funds for higher education were not plentiful, and he considered it important to discuss the matter with deans and department heads. At about the same time, Coffman began inviting the leadership of the faculty senate to the national "Faculty Roles and Rewards" meetings of the American Association of Higher Education. By encouraging participation in each of these settings, the provost helped set the stage for productive discussions between the administration and the faculty on issues critical to the life of the university.

According to Coffman, it was also important to the process that the university had spent several years on its own adjusting the annual evaluation process before the regents' call for new policies and practices for faculty performance reviews. In 1991, the board of regents established a task force for improving faculty evaluation, bringing together a broad-based group that included one member of the board, two chief academic officers from the Kansas system, two faculty members, two students, and two members of the regents' professional staff. The group produced a general statement on faculty evaluation in 1992. During the years 1990 through 1993, K-State revised its promotion and tenure policies, overlapping with the board of regents' task force efforts. While each department developed its own standards and criteria, each college established an advisory committee to evaluate these standards and criteria. In addition, the college advisory committees were charged with reviewing candidates for promotion and tenure and with making recommendations to their deans for each candidate. Provost Coffman believes the collaborative environment that the board, faculty, and administration cultivated over these years was essential to developing the new policy.

John Heibert, a cardiologist and new chair of the Kansas Board of Regents, visited K-State around the same time as the board's list of recommendations for greater accountability arrived on campus. As an adjunct clinical professor at the University of Kansas, he was perhaps better positioned to make the regents' case than the previous chair who was a banker and a businessman. Former faculty senate president, and dean of the College of Technology and Aviation at K-State's Salina Campus, Dennis Kuhlman, recalled that during his visit, Heibert reiterated the regents' conviction that some level "of 'deadwood' [existed] throughout the university system."

The provost's first step after release of the recommendations was to give the faculty senate a chance to address the board's concerns. Stepping to one side, he asked faculty leaders to guide the effort. He recalled, "I said, 'What is the faculty going to do about this?' The senate president replied, 'We'll step up to the plate.'" One policy objective, as the provost described it, would be to "nudge the driftwood into action," while another would be to establish a means for reallocating effort among faculty members.

From the outset, Provost Coffman paid close attention to the political aspects of the process. The president and provost met with the leadership of the faculty senate every month. He said another crucial element was that KSU "had three [consecutive] senate presidents who believed in this evaluation process." Coffman noted, "You can't just say 'here's the plan.' It takes time. You have to wade into the thicket, get faculty to buy in, then work through the decision-making process." He added that the significant tenure of K-State administrators was also valuable: "If I had only been here three to five years, this would never have been accomplished."

The Chronic Low Achievers Task Force

In fall 1995, then-Faculty Senate President Kuhlman formed a special task force to address the call for a new policy. The task force of seven included primarily faculty members, as well as department heads, and one dean. The group was charged with reviewing existing policies and procedures to ensure that: (a) assistance is provided for faculty renewal and development; (b) an adequate definition of chronic low performance is included in evaluation, promotion, and tenure criteria guidelines; and (c) dismissal policies include provisions for including chronic low performance as an indicator of incompetence.

To this point, discussions about the regents' resolution and chronic low achievement policies had not been especially heated. However, many faculty leaders raised a furor when the regents suggested that chronic low achievers could be identified from a list of faculty who had repeatedly received low salary increases. In view of the fact that the university had lacked the funds to offer significant salary increases in recent years, many faculty members viewed this proposal as flawed and unfair. According to Kuhlman, the regents wanted to label "anyone who had less than a 1 percent raise as deadwood." He said, "We refuted that by reminding them that all university raises had been small in the first place, and for that reason it was possible for a productive faculty member to receive a small raise." A member of the Faculty Affairs Committee, Associate Professor of Agronomy Gary Pierzynski, described the regents' proposal as a turning point for faculty leaders. It was clear that "if *we* didn't do something, the regents would do something to us."

Pierzynski, chair of the Chronic Low Achievers Task Force, said, "We began by examining the regents' memo and decided that we wanted to avoid a full-blown post-tenure review policy," which he described as a repeated retenuring process that would force tenured faculty members to continually reapply for their jobs. While recognizing that the university needed to respond to the concerns expressed by the board of regents, the committee wanted to find a middle ground, stopping short of extreme measures that might change the nature of faculty appointments or the faculty culture at K-State.

The task force went to work, conducting a wide-ranging review of existing faculty evaluation policies in departments and colleges across the university. The group then drafted a policy statement on chronic low achievement intended to put pressure on department heads to conduct more systematic annual evaluations and to document them in a substantive manner that would serve multiple purposes. By August 1995, the Chronic Low Achievers Task Force asked the Faculty Affairs Committee to consider the newly drafted language on chronic low achievers as a proposed addition to the faculty handbook.

Negotiating New Measures

In meetings of the Faculty Affairs Committee and the full faculty senate, the strongest opponents to the notion of a policy to address low faculty performance argued that it was an infringement on the rights earned by tenured faculty members. Kuhlman recalled that some faculty protested ardently on the grounds that "any comprehensive evaluation after the tenuring process is tantamount to revoking tenure." Physics Department Head James Legg said he and others were vehemently opposed "because of what it does to faculty morale. It sends the wrong message."

At the other end of the spectrum, a faculty senator who helped shepherd the new policy through the approval channels described the resistors as a particularly cynical lot that "went as far as to say 'This will be the death of tenure.'" Likewise, David Balk, another former senate president, now head of the Department of Family Relations and Child Development at Oklahoma State University, argued that, contrary to the views of some dissidents, "tenure is not an entitlement to be nonproductive. Tenure protects academic freedom, but we cannot hide behind tenure to cover low productivity."

Still other faculty leaders pointed out that the university already employed multiple layers of evaluation. The minutes of the December 12, 1995, faculty senate meeting state: "Senator Michie believes the Faculty Handbook and the AAUP Guidelines provide sufficient protection for the university in cases of low achievement by tenured faculty. She suggested we should simply tell the Regents that 'We're already covered.'" As Physics Department Head James Legg put it, "Our faculty are already evaluated so thoroughly, there's no place to hide."

Some faculty believed the real problem was "public relations and public image," namely, misperceptions among the public and the legislature about what faculty members do. Former Senate President Balk commented, "Most people don't understand what faculty do. We haven't done a good job of telling them." In addition, Kuhlman noted, "There's a nationwide misperception that there's a lot of deadwood on the faculty."

Others were particularly offended by the suggestion that there are large numbers of unproductive faculty members at K-State. Pierzynski argued that the situation, in fact, was just the opposite:

"I work in a department of chronic overachievers—highly competitive and productive." To this point, Kuhlman added that the term "average" becomes "extremely difficult to define. Faculty who find themselves in a small department surrounded with overachievers are severely penalized by an emphasis on merit."

Shared Governance in Action: Enacting a New Policy

After months of spirited discussion, debate, and negotiation, the language drafted by the task force moved through the Faculty Affairs Committee (responsible for formulating polices on matters such as faculty employment, tenure, promotions, and workload). The minutes of the faculty senate meeting in December 1995 record that "Senator Pierzynski moved to approve new faculty handbook section C31.5. An amended version of the policy passed with a vote of 45 'yes' and 23 'no.'"

How was the faculty senate ultimately able to pass a "chronic low achievers policy"? The provost attributed the policy's passage to close collaboration between the administration and the faculty. Professor Kuhlman echoed this view, stating, "K-State has a shared governance system that operates at a high level. It works as a result of open communication." In a similar vein, the regents praised the "sincere cooperation of the faculty senate presidents," and a senate president, in turn, complimented the regents, describing them as "intelligent participants."

However, not everyone painted such a rosy picture. Philosophy Department Head Hamilton, who counted himself among the strong opponents to the new policy, described the situation as more divisive: "My colleagues work very hard, yet the regents are telling us 'We don't care what you say, we want to find out who's not doing anything.' We were simply told to create a policy, irrespective of the real situation at hand." Hamilton pointed out that the faculty senate is comprised of approximately two-thirds faculty and one-third staff and administrators, and that when it came to a vote, about one-half of the faculty members who served on the senate voted against C31.5. Another department head remarked that he and his colleagues were "burned and embittered by the whole thing."

Still others attributed passage of the policy to political realities. That is, the issue was not whether there would be a policy, but rather who would write it. Drafting the policy in the senate was a means of taking the matter into "our own hands rather than allowing something to be done to us." If the faculty had not addressed the board's concerns, it is very likely that the regents would have proceeded anyway, and perhaps even have adopted a comprehensive post-tenure review policy. "We didn't need C31.5 to say that incompetence is unacceptable," Professor Legg commented. "We needed it because the regents felt that they needed it from every university in the system, to show the legislature that we're not sheltering unproductive faculty with tenure." At the December 12, 1995, faculty senate meeting Senate President Kuhlman explained that "the BOR staff and some members had reviewed our faculty handbook. They did not think our [policy on] 'incompetence' covered 'chronic low achievers.' We needed something to satisfy the regents and the public."

A statement on chronic low achievement was, in the minds of many, a lesser evil than a board-crafted policy on chronic low achievement or worse, a full-scale post-tenure review system. From that perspective, observed a former senate president, the new policy was "a means to safeguard tenure." Moreover, he commented, in order to sell the policy, "we pointed out that we believed there would be very few professors who [would] fall into that [below-minimum-standards] category." Whatever the mix of motives and rationales, a new policy was enacted.

The Result

> C31.5. *Chronic Low Achievement.* Chronic failure of a tenured faculty member to perform his or her professional duties, as defined in the respective unit, shall con-

stitute evidence of "professional incompetence" and war-
rant consideration for "dismissal for cause" under existing university policies. Each department or unit shall
develop a set of guidelines describing the minimum
acceptable level of productivity for all applicable areas
of responsibility for the faculty, as well as procedures to
handle such cases. In keeping with regular procedures in
matters of tenure (C112.1 and C112.2), eligible departmental faculty will have input into any decision on individual cases unless the faculty member requests
otherwise. When a tenured faculty member's overall performance falls below the minimum acceptable level, as
indicated by the annual evaluation, the department or
unit head shall indicate so in writing to the faculty member. The department head will also indicate, in writing, a
suggested course of action to improve the performance
of the faculty member. In subsequent annual evaluations,
the faculty member will report on activities aimed at
improving performance and any evidence of improvement. The names of faculty members who fail to meet
minimum standards for the year following the department head's suggested course of action will be forwarded
to the appropriate dean. If the faculty member has two
successive evaluations or a total of three evaluations in
any five-year period in which minimum standards are not
met, then "dismissal for cause" will be considered at the
discretion of the appropriate dean [Excerpted from the
Kansas State University Faculty Handbook, Section C:
Faculty Identity, Employment, and Tenure].

Local Autonomy for Academic Departments

A critical element of the new policy was delegation of defining the
guidelines for determining a "minimum acceptable level of productivity. . .as well as procedures to handle such cases" to individual

academic departments. The faculty members of each department, working as a group, were to devise standards and evaluation criteria for minimum acceptable performance. Department heads were given the responsibility to identify the point at which this threshold had been crossed, to set in motion remediation activities to address the situation, and if necessary, to determine the point at which dismissal for cause might be considered. The policy was structured so that in a case where Section C31.5 was triggered, the faculty member in question would be given at least one year, and potentially as many as four years, to improve his or her performance before dismissal for cause could be considered.

By early 1997, department heads and faculty members began adapting their performance evaluation practices to comply with Section C31.5. While Provost Coffman described this provision as "fundamental to implementation of C31.5," he also stated "this will vary, consistent with departments' evaluation systems. Consequently, there will be many approaches that will accomplish this task. . .Some departments have adopted a quantitative approach, while others have chosen a more qualitative approach. Neither method will be rejected on that basis alone" (Letter to Deans on March 12, 1997). Of greater concern to the provost was that the policies be clear, even-handed, and consistent with the university's performance expectations of faculty.

The faculty made a conscious decision to have departments develop their own standards because, as Pierzynski noted, "they know their disciplines best." John Havlin, former faculty senate president, described this provision as a key component of the new policy and one that enabled C31.5 to gain approval. However, in the faculty senate meeting of June 11, 1997, Senator Aruna Michie pointed out that "individuals and departments are not totally free to set standards, since departmental standards, at least, must be approved by the deans and the provost." The possibility of uniform, university-wide standards was raised but deemed infeasible in the same meeting because "K-State's departments and colleges had very different missions, and therefore very different job descriptions."

Balk remarked, "The provost and the deans will help make the differences between departments equitable." However, the potential for taking advantage of the department's prerogative cropped up early in the process of developing guidelines, when Balk observed that "in some departments there was an effort to make expectations so low that no one could fail them." Noting the disparities between departmental standards, some faculty members began to wonder whether the system could work fairly.

In 1997–1998, each department drafted guidelines for minimum acceptable levels of productivity and submitted them to the provost's office for initial review by Jane Rowlett, Director of Unclassified Affairs and University Compliance. In the first round, Coffman and Rowlett returned draft guidelines to nearly two-thirds of the departments for additional work. According to Coffman, most of the unacceptable drafts were returned because they failed to adequately address the question of "what to do when a faculty member is failing or fallow in one major area [but not in other areas]." Other drafts failed to describe the department's means of triggering the C31.5 process.

Some departments defined minimum standards in a very broad way, while others enumerated tasks and set acceptable percentages of completion. Table 1 at the end of this chapter outlines policy proposals from three departments. The guidelines for one natural science department were very specific and rigorous, while a social science department's minimum standards were vague and skeletal. Between these extremes, a department in agriculture used an evaluation process whereby "the head rates faculty on each applicable criterion (examples include teaching improvement, research focus and aggressiveness, and peer evaluations) and develops an overall rating in each of the following categories: teaching, research, extension, nondirected service, and directed service activities." The final merit score was weighted according to the percentage of effort devoted to each area. An overall rating of less than 60 on a 100-point scale in any of the four categories would indicate failure to achieve the minimum acceptable level of productivity.

There was no clear consensus on whether any one approach to defining minimum standards would be most effective. Rowlett pointed out that while the evaluation procedures that relied heavily on a formula to identify productivity levels appeared to be very thorough, some faculty and administrators worried that this method might dampen creativity or discourage interdisciplinary scholarship and teaching. Concern was especially high where the criteria explicitly rewarded scholarly publications only in certain disciplinary journals.

Interpreting "Scripture"

Rather than marking the end of a successful round of policymaking, the passage of Section C31.5, in fact, opened a new series of discussions about the point at which the policy would be invoked. On January 8, 1996, Coffman wrote a memo to the university's deans describing how the new faculty evaluation process should be implemented:

> Department Heads are to meet individually with each faculty member . . . for the purpose of establishing, in general terms, the distribution of the faculty member's time and effort for the coming year, and what the expectations should reasonably be as to performance standards and criteria. The results of this discussion should be specific and unique for the individual, and consistent with more general criteria and standards which should exist in each department's document on criteria and standards for evaluation, promotion, and tenure. Any problem areas which exist from the previous year(s) should also be clarified, along with a plan for addressing them.
>
> At the conclusion of the year, the annual merit

evaluation is to include, along with whatever other numerical ratings and narrative, an overall assessment of "meets expectations, exceeds expectations, or fails to meet expectations." Thus, we will cease to compare faculty with each other, and instead compare performance with individualized expectations . . . Salary adjustment is then reconciled with each of these groups, with the general assumption that "fails to meet expectations" will result in no salary increase.

During this period, the provost met frequently with the Council of Deans, department heads, and faculty leaders, including the Faculty Affairs Committee. In February 1996 he presented a series of workshops for deans, associate deans, and department heads on faculty evaluation as related to the new policy on chronic low achievement. While Coffman was pleased with the "level of ideas and interaction that took place" in the workshops, he also recognized the need to clarify the definition of what would constitute an overall rating of "below expectations."

In Coffman's view, the assignment of responsibilities and setting of goals for each faculty member was primarily a resource allocation process. With this in mind, on February 22, 1996, he wrote to deans and department heads, stating: "In instances where one or *more critical*, or *essential*, areas of an individual's work (consistent with the department's document on criteria and standards) are found to fall below expectations, the *overall* [emphasis added] evaluation should be considered to fall below expectations. This means that if a person is consistently falling below expectations in a critical area of work, by definition we are wasting the resources attached to that activity." The provost explained further that if this situation occurred, Section C31.5 would trigger "a serious assessment of the individual's role in the department, as well as the establishment of a meaningful remediation development plan."

Coffman's interpretation was highly controversial. The contention that, if a small percentage of a faculty member's appointment—for instance, a 20 percent assignment to research—were deemed substandard, the entire evaluation would be considered substandard, "evoked a real firestorm," according to Balk. Professor Legg voiced the fear among some faculty members that a department might "force a small percentage of responsibility in an area that the faculty member cannot meet." The faculty senate meeting minutes for April 9, 1996, reported:

> Faculty Affairs met just prior to the Senate meeting with Provost Coffman to discuss section C31.5 of the Faculty Handbook, as requested by the Senate. Specific questions regarded the Provost's call for individualized faculty evaluations, under which a faculty member not meeting his/her expectations would not be given a raise, even though s/he meets minimum department standards. In addition, he specified that "chronic low achievement" referred to failure to meet one or more standards deemed "critical" in the department's mission statement. Senators expressed concern about the seeming variance from the Senate's specification for "overall" performance. Senator Robert Poresky voiced his concern about a faculty member with a 10 percent service "goal" and no time to fulfill it, in which case a strict reading of "overall" would mean that the entire evaluation, however excellent the other components, would be below minimum standards.

For some faculty, the discussion took on the tenor of a turf battle, and the provost's interpretation of the new policy was viewed as aggressive interference. In the April faculty senate meeting, Pierzynski said Provost Coffman had "'drawn a line in the sand' with the strict reading of the term 'overall'" and reiterated Senator Jennifer Kassebaum's suggestion after the last senate meeting that "perhaps the provost might like to only 'recommend' that interpretation."

In an attempt to clarify these issues from the faculty's perspective, Faculty Senator Pierzynski described four areas of faculty concern in a letter to the provost on April 21, 1996. First, Pierzynski stated that a "clear separation of the individualized evaluation approach, in which a person is deemed to have either failed to meet, met or exceeded expectations, and the chronic [low] achievement issue is essential." The second point of concern was related to realistic goal setting. The letter outlined two possible situations: a faculty member setting low goals that could easily be exceeded, or at the other end of the spectrum, a department head establishing "unattainable goals that a person would always fail to meet, despite tremendous effort." Third, Pierzynski suggested that the provost had overinterpreted Section C31.5 by construing failure in one critical or essential area to signify "overall" failure. The final concern related to the plan to use faculty evaluations as a mechanism for resource reallocation. Pierzynski stated, "many have expressed concern about flexibility in changing appointments of those who are not performing well in a particular area. Such changes in appointments can influence an entire department if important areas of teaching, research, or extension are not being covered or become the responsibility of a few individuals."

The provost responded four days later, steadfastly maintaining his position. Before discussing the senate's specific concerns, Coffman made two points: "(1) The only new provision in this entire process is the establishment of 'minimum standards' called for in C31.5. Everything else is in place. (2) Moving to an individualized system of evaluation is first, and foremost, based upon issues related to resource allocation . . . it is essential to engendering more flexible allocation of time and effort." With these observations, Coffman cut to what he saw as the heart of the matter. The real objective of this new approach was "to optimize the likelihood of all faculty being fully productive, and eliminating waste of resources as represented by underutilized time."

The provost commented on each of the faculty senate's concerns. First, he stated that there was no real separation between individual goals and expectations and the minimum departmental standards because the minimum standards should be "understood in the context of each individual's annual game plan." Regarding the use of the term "overall," the provost maintained the position that unsatisfactory performance in one critical or essential area would lead to a below-standard overall evaluation: "At some point, the degree of inadequacy in a given area of work, essential to the mission of the department, is severe enough that corrective action must be taken. For example, at present, we have individuals who have 20 or 30 percent of their assignment in research, and their research productivity is zero. In most instances, their overall evaluation is described as satisfactory and no action is taken. This should cause the entire evaluation to be below minimum standards."

Taking up the topic of reallocation of time and responsibilities, the provost agreed with Pierzynski that in some cases and some departments, this process would be complex and other faculty work might be affected. He allowed that in some cases, reallocation of time would not be feasible and at that point, a "plan for development of requisite skills [would] be part of the department head's 'suggested course of action to improve the performance of the faculty member.'" Finally, with regard to assuring that realistic goals would be established, the provost noted, "specific safeguards are in place to prevent abuse, and must be observed." These included checkpoints at which a faculty member could see his/her evaluation before it was sent to the next level, and ultimately, to the university's grievance process.

Clarifying C31.5

The discussions between the provost and the faculty leadership continued through the spring term and into the fall of 1996. After months of wrangling over the definition of "overall," and the point at which the policy would be invoked, faculty leaders drafted three addenda to the new policy. On December 10, 1996, the senate approved Sections C31.6, C31.7, and C.31.8 (See Exhibit 2). As Kuhlman described it, these measures were added "because some felt a need to limit C31.5."

The issue of separating minimum department standards from individual expectations was addressed in Section C31.6, which states: "'dismissal for cause' in cases of professional incompetence can only be based on departmental guidelines about minimum acceptable levels of performance that apply generally to all members of the department or unit and are distinct from individually determined annual goals." In addition, C31.6 emphasized that minimum acceptable levels of performance and the definition of the term "productivity" would be the province of each department. In fact, departments were given considerable leeway. As noted in Section C31.6, "It is expected that guidelines concerning minimum acceptable levels of productivity will vary considerably from unit to unit."

Section C31.7 explicitly stipulated that before any faculty member could be dismissed for cause, serious attempts at remediation must have taken place. It called for a written record of evaluations signaling deficient performance. Only after these had occurred could the department head and the faculty member agree to a reallocation of responsibilities.

Finally, C31.8 detailed the terminology to be used for annual evaluations, with the term "minimum acceptable levels of productivity" referring to the minimum standards called for in C31.5. When approved in December 1996, the text of C31.8 called for departmental guidelines to "explicitly state the point at which a faculty member's overall performance can bring C31.5 into play. The guidelines should reflect the common and dictionary meaning of 'overall' as 'comprehensive.'" In May 1998, the administration and faculty senate renegotiated this section, softening the language somewhat. Rather than "explicitly state the point" at which C31.5 would be brought into play, the guidelines were required to "clearly explain how the department or unit will determine when a tenured faculty member's low performance in one or more instances fails overall to meet the minimum acceptable level."

Practical Effects

Views among administrators and faculty members varied regarding what the new chronic low achievement policy would accomplish. For Coffman, the policy was a mechanism for "nudging the drift-wood into action" and a tool that would allow the university to real-locate faculty time and effort when necessary. The regents also appeared to be pleased with the results. John Welsh, the Executive Director of the Board of Regents, said, "The regents believe that we now have policies in place that will allow for the dismissal of chronic low performers, because there will be a clear, written record of evaluation and efforts toward remediation."

Kuhlman viewed the new system and policy as "a success already, because I see a change in attitude. You can no longer go to the department head and say, 'I'm working on a book.' Now you can expect to be asked when it will be finished and how it's being used to enhance teaching." Another former faculty senate president, Havlin, spoke proudly of C31.5: "We stood up and said unproduc-tive faculty members are unacceptable. We stood up and did some-thing about it."

Others predicted that the new policy would have very little effect on the way faculty conduct their work. Instead, they said it had symbolic and political value. Pierzynski predicted that C31.5 would not bring about any major changes. "What the university got out of this is good public relations," he commented. Another fac-ulty senate member called the policy "something to impress the leg-islature. It's hard for me to see any other major benefit."

Neither the faculty, nor the administration or board expected the chronic low achievement policy to produce large numbers of pink slips. In fact, the provost estimated that there might be as few as three to five dismissals over ten years. Welsh, the executive director of the board, predicted that fewer than ten professors would be terminated for cause over that time. He asserted that the regents' "genuine objective is improvement, not dismissal. They are interested in using it as leverage."

By spring 1998, departments had identified seven cases in which faculty members were not meeting the department's definition of minimum acceptable levels of productivity. Specifically, none were producing research. Of the seven, one faculty member chose to retire, two have undergone a reallocation of efforts, two developed remedial plans of action, and another two improved their performance sufficiently to meet the minimum departmental standards. If any of these faculty members fails to meet standards in 1999, the C31.5 remediation process could come into play.

Questions on the Horizon

In April 1998, as K-State's departments continued to develop and refine new evaluation formats and minimum performance standards in consultation with Provost Coffman, some faculty leaders reflected on the results of their work and the questions it raised about the future.

One question was whether the board of regents would be satisfied with an approach that encourages remediation and would likely produce few, if any, pink slips. Had the faculty adequately shored up the dike, was it buying time, or could it be sowing the seeds of further intervention by the board?

Others asked whether the new policy would be effective with such disparate standards among the departments. Was it fair and feasible for some departments to have explicit and stringent standards while others were more nebulous and lenient? What would happen if faculty members in units with rigorous standards suffered adverse consequences, while faculty members in other units did not? And finally, would tenure be safer, or less so, as a result of the policy changes?

In a similar vein, Professor Brad Fenwick in the College of Veterinary Medicine foresaw a possible problem with the concept of reallocating faculty resources. He predicted, "If one person is a mediocre teacher and, as a result of the new process, his appointment is adjusted so that he is assigned 80 percent research and less teaching, then another person in the same department might be ticked off at having to teach an extra course. It might even be incentive for some to teach poorly in order to get out from under a heavy teaching load."

A number of K-State's faculty leaders and administrators offered their early conjectures. Some said, "Yes, we have averted an attempt at establishing post-tenure review." Kuhlman declared, "Tenure has not been challenged. Rather, the ability to use tenure as a shield from productivity and accountability has been challenged." An administrator commented, "The C31.5 process saved the university from evaluating every single faculty member in a full post-tenure review process by only dealing with chronic low achievers." Others disagreed. Professor Hamilton remarked, "Tenure is now *less* secure—and the university needs tenure to attract a high-quality faculty. Now we are at risk of opening the door to an assault on tenure." For many, however, the effect of the chronic low achievement policy on tenure remained an open question—one that only time and future events will answer.

Exhibit 1. Memorandum on Faculty Evaluation Recommendations

March 23, 1995

MEMORANDUM

TO: Members, Council of Presidents
FROM: Stephen M. Jordan, Executive Director
RE: Faculty Evaluation Recommendations

At the March 16, 1995 Board meeting, the Board of Regents acted on the one remaining recommendation pertaining to faculty evaluation. The recommendations adopted in December 1994 and

Exhibit 1. Memorandum on Faculty Evaluation Recommendations, cont'd.

March 1995 supplement recommendations adopted in April 1992. I have attached copies of the recommendations the Board expects to be implemented in this important area of our accountability to the public. Please note that the Board expects a report on the implementation of these recommendations in May 1996. I have also enclosed a draft of the student perceptions of instruction survey instrument the Board endorsed in March. The councils should react to this draft prior to the Board's consideration of it in May. Once it is adopted, each institution will need to develop a plan to implement it in the 1995–1996 academic year.

cc: Members, Kansas Board of Regents
    Members, Council of Chief Academic Officers
    Members, Council of Faculty Senate Presidents

FACULTY EVALUATION RECOMMENDATIONS

1a. Teaching faculty should be rated by students at least once a year, on a form that is controlled for student motivation and other possible bias. The form should contain directions which indicate how the information is used, and the forms should be administered and collected under controlled conditions that assure students' anonymity. Each academic unit should determine the student rating form to be used by its faculty that conform to the above guidelines.

1b. Multiple sources of information should be gathered to evaluate teaching. Sources of information might include the content of the course, its design and presentation. For example, (a) syllabi, examinations and samples of graded exams, textbooks, etc. might be evaluated by peers for their suitability and coherence, (b) videos of class presentations might be viewed by peers or the department chair to evaluate presentation of material, etc.

Exhibit 1. Memorandum on Faculty Evaluation Recommendations, cont'd.

Units should be encouraged to develop a comprehensive, flexible approach to teaching evaluation that includes several types of evidence that can be collected, presented and evaluated as a portfolio. Student ratings of teaching should be an important part of this portfolio; they are nevertheless only one part. Peer evaluation, defined as a comprehensive, critical review by knowledgeable colleagues of each faculty member's entire range of teaching activities, should be the foundation of the university's teaching evaluation program. No single course of information, including ratings by students, should be taken at face value, but rather should be interpreted by those peers who are in the best position to understand this evidence and to place it in the appropriate academic context. Departments should be encouraged to use additional tools such as exit interviews and graduate interviews and surveys to obtain information about teaching effectiveness.

2a. All department chairs should participate in the evaluation of faculty and meet with faculty individually as needed to discuss the evaluation. Institutions should enhance opportunities for the preparation of department chairs for work in departmental administration, particularly as that relates to the evaluation of faculty and the allocation of faculty effort as in (4).

2b. At the beginning of each academic year, representatives from Student Governance on each campus should have the opportunity to meet with campus representatives from Academic Affairs or their designees to discuss the operation of student ratings of teaching. Ratings of individual faculty are not an appropriate subject in such discussions.

3. Instruments to measure student ratings of instruction should solicit, at a minimum, student perspectives on (a) the delivery of instruction, (b) the assessment of learning, (c) the availability of the faculty members to students, and (d) whether the goals and objectives of the course were met. Printed directions

Exhibit 1. Memorandum on Faculty Evaluation Recommendations, cont'd.

on the rating scale should indicate that the information will be used by the individual faculty member to improve his or her instruction. The department, college and university will also use the information to enhance teaching effectiveness. The forms should be determined, administered, and collected under controlled conditions that assure student anonymity, as indicated in Recommendations 1a and 1b.

4.   Based upon institutional and departmental goals, tenured and tenure-track faculty should meet with their department chair individually to allocate the amount of effort that faculty member will devote to teaching, research and service. A reduction of effort in one area should be made up by augmentation in another. Merit evaluation of faculty should follow this agreement. These agreements should reflect varying emphases at different times within a faculty member's career. Teaching should be evaluated as rigorously as research.

5.   All campuses should insure that each school or college develops a plan to financially recognize faculty who are promoted.

6.   In FY 1995, data should be provided on the number and percentage of faculty who received 0% to 1% for the past three consecutive years, and the percentage of all faculty who received a 0% and 1% raise in each of the three past years. This information must be viewed in the context of the total dollars available for merit raises; therefore, the amount of General Fund increase for merit raises should also be given for each of the past three years.

7a.   Each campus should i) provide assistance for faculty renewal and development, ii) define chronic low performance, and iii) examine dismissal policies to include chronic low performance, *despite all assistance*, as an indicator of incompetence.

7b.   Each institution should provide information to the Board on

Exhibit 1. Memorandum on Faculty Evaluation Recommendations, cont'd.

efforts to improve teaching. The Board will distribute with student ratings scales a one-page survey of student perceptions of instruction. The survey will be collected separately from the student ratings scales used in the evaluation of faculty. The survey will be used to demonstrate student attitudes toward instruction at the Regents universities.

The Regents universities should provide the Board with a report by June 1996 on the implementation of the recommendations adopted in December 1994 and March 1995.

ADOPTED BY THE KANSAS BOARD OF REGENTS, MARCH 16, 1995.

Exhibit 2. Excerpt from the Kansas State Faculty Handbook, Section C: Faculty Identity, Employment, Tenure

C31.6 Section C31.5 is about revocation of tenure in individual cases. Tenure is essential for the protection of the independence of the teaching and research faculty in institutions of higher learning in the United States. Decisions about revocation of tenure, especially if the grounds are professional incompetence, should not be exclusively controlled or determined by and should not be unduly influenced by single individuals without input from faculty. Moreover, "dismissal for cause" in cases of professional incompetence can only be based on departmental guidelines about minimum-acceptable levels of performance that apply generally to all members of the department or unit and are distinct from individually determined annual goals. Consequently, C31.5 establishes a departmental and faculty procedure for the decision about the revocation of tenure for professional incompetence. It is not the purpose of C31.5

**Exhibit 2. Excerpt from the Kansas State Faculty Handbook,
Section C: Faculty Identity, Employment, Tenure, cont'd.**

to promote, endorse, encourage, or to have any stand whatsoever
on the definition of "productivity," its relation to publication, or the
proper relationship between measurable definitions of productivity
and an intellectual University environment that is favorable to substantive scholarship, long-range projects, or critical and creative
thinking. These are matters that C31.5 leaves to the department or
unit to consider in "developing a set of guidelines describing the
minimum-acceptable level of productivity for all applicable areas of
responsibility." These minimum standards are not the same as those
referred to in C31.1 or C41.1. It is expected that guidelines concerning minimum-acceptable levels of productivity will vary considerable from unit to unit. Not only disciplinary differences but
differences in philosophies of departmental administration are
appropriate. What is not appropriate is the undue protection of
non-contributing members of the faculty.

C31.7 Prior to the point at which "dismissal for cause" is considered under C31.5, other less drastic actions should have been taken.
In most cases, the faculty member's deficient performance ("below
expectations" or worse) in one or more areas of responsibility will
have been noted in prior annual evaluations. At that point, the first
responsibility of the head of the department or unit is to determine
explicitly whether the duties assigned to the faculty member have
been equitable in the context of the distribution of duties within
the unit and to correct any inequities affecting the faculty member
under review. Second, the head of the department or unit should
have offered the types of assistance indicated in C30.3. Referral for
still other forms of assistance (e.g., medical or psychological) may
be warranted. Third, if the deficient performance continues in spite
of these efforts and recommendations, the department head and the

**Exhibit 2. Excerpt from the Kansas State Faculty Handbook,
Section C: Faculty Identity, Employment, Tenure, cont'd.**

faculty member may agree to a reallocation of the faculty member's time so that he/she no longer has duties in the area(s) of deficient performance. Of course, such reallocation can occur only if there are one or more areas of better performance in the faculty member's profile and if the reallocation is possible in the larger context of the department's or unit's mission, needs, and resources.

C31.8 To help clarify the relationship between annual evaluations for merit, salary, and promotion and evaluations that could lead to C31.5, the following recommendations are made:

a. When annual evaluations are stated in terms of "expectations," then the categories should include at least the following: "exceeded expectations," "met expectations," "fallen below expectations but has met minimum-acceptable levels of productivity," and "fallen below minimum-acceptable levels of productivity," with the "minimum-acceptable levels of productivity" referring to the minimum standards called for in C31.5.

b. The department's or unit's guidelines for "minimum-acceptable levels of productivity" should explicitly state the point at which a faculty member's overall performance can bring C31.5 into play. The guidelines should reflect the common and dictionary meaning of "overall" as "comprehensive," which may be based on any of the following:

1. A certain percentage of total responsibilities
2. Number of areas of responsibility
3. Weaknesses not balanced by strengths
4. Predetermined agreements with the faculty member about the relative importance of different areas of responsibility

Table 1. Minimum Performance Standards

	Department in Natural Sciences / Social Sciences	Department	Department in
in Agriculture / Overall Concept	The department developed a proportionality system that accounts for differences in assigned effort to teaching, research, extension, and service (0 percent to 100 percent in a given area). Faculty are rated on a five-point performance scale (1=unsatisfactory, 5=excellent). Performance ratings are multiplied by the proportion of effort assigned (for example, a 70 percent teaching assignment rated at 3.6 would be calculated as 3.6 x 0.7). A grand score is obtained by adding the ratings for each area. A final score is obtained by adjusting the grand score by the faculty member's salary relative to other salaries in the department. "A faculty member with a higher salary is expected to have a proportionally higher productivity."	The department head assigns a score for each performance category (including nondirected service for all and extension, teaching, research, and directed service according to the individual appointment). The department head subjectively determines levels of accomplishment based on careful consideration of standards for particular criteria in each category. A five-point rating scale is used in which 1=unsatisfactory and 5=excellent. After rating a faculty member on each criterion, the head determines an overall rating on a scale of 0 to 100 in each category. The department guideline states that "faculty who receive a performance rating of less than 60 in teaching, research, extension, or directed service fail to achieve the minimal acceptable level of productivity."	The statements below comprise the department's definition of minimum performance standards.
Teaching	Minimum expectations are "one course taught every 4 years for each 0.1 appointment assigned to teaching. . . with TEVAL	The minimum standard is an overall rating of 60 in teaching. Examples of criteria and standards for teaching include: student evaluations; TEVAL scores; evaluations by head or assistant head (classroom visits, review of teaching materials); and the quantity and quality of graduate acad-	The minimum standard is stated as: "Fulfills assigned teaching duties."

	scores averaging 2.5 (on a scale of 1–5 with 5 as best) . . . Consideration is given to those classes that do not fill for reasons beyond the control of the teacher. . .or for other special reasons."	emic advising based on interviews conducted by department head.	The minimum standard is stated as: "Progress shown."
Research and Publication	"For research appointments of 0.7 and above, two refereed articles over the past 4 years is considered a minimal expectation. For research appointments of 0.1 or 0.2 (primarily Extension faculty) one refereed article over the past 5 years is considered a minimal expectation."	The minimum standard is an overall rating of 60 for research. Criteria and standards include: level of research focus and aggressiveness in attaining goals; quantity and quality of refereed publications; and level of extramural funding.	Not rated.
Extension	Minimum expectations for extension appointments are an "average score of at least 3 (on a scale of 1–5, with 5 as best) on the annual County Agent evaluation of their performance," which examines the quantity, quality, and reputation of their work.	The minimum standard is a rating of 60 for extension. Criteria and standards for extension include quantity and quality of program development and implementation; peer evaluations of meetings, tours, or demonstrations; level of teamwork and client relationships; and quantity and quality of extension publications.	
Service	Not rated.	The minimum standard for nondirected service is a rating of 60. Criteria and standards for nondirected service include contributions through committee assignments; participation in profession-based service and recognition; professional contributions to government or civic groups; and the extent of private consulting activities.	Minimum standards are stated as: "Departmental and university service: Carries share of duties." "Professional service: Participates actively in the profession." "Community service: Responds to requests for service from off campus."

Index